Y0-DAM-462

KETO DIET
AIR FRYER

Cookbook for Beginners

Easy, Healthy, Mouthwatering Recipes
to Limit Carbohydrates and Maximize Health

Peter Bragg

Text Copyright © Peter Bragg

All rights reserved. No part of this guide may be reproduced in any form without permission in writing from the publisher except in the case of brief quotations embodied in critical articles or reviews.

Legal & Disclaimer

The information contained in this book and its contents is not designed to replace or take the place of any form of medical or professional advice; and is not meant to replace the need for independent medical, financial, legal or other professional advice or services, as may be required. The content and information in this book have been provided for educational and entertainment purposes only.The content and information contained in this book have been compiled from sources deemed reliable, and it is accurate to the best of the Author's knowledge, information, and belief.

However, the Author cannot guarantee its accuracy and validity and cannot be held liable for any errors and/or omissions. Further, changes are periodically made to this book as and when needed. Where appropriate and/or necessary, you must consult a professional (including but not limited to your doctor, attorney, financial advisor or such other professional advisor) before using any of the suggested remedies, techniques, or information in this book.

Upon using the contents and information contained in this book, you agree to hold harmless the Author from and against any damages, costs, and expenses, including any legal fees potentially resulting from the application of any of the information provided by this book. This disclaimer applies to any loss, damages or injury caused by the use and application, whether directly or indirectly, of any advice or information presented, whether for breach of contract, tort, negligence, personal injury, criminal intent, or under any other cause of action.

You agree to accept all risks of using the information presented inside this book.

You agree that by continuing to read this book, where appropriate and/or necessary, you shall consult a professional (including but not limited to your doctor, attorney, or financial advisor or such other advisor as needed) before using any of the suggested remedies, techniques, or information in this book.

Table of Contents

Description

Trying out a new diet is an exciting moment, but it can be quite stressful at the same time. There will be things that you will have to increase, remove, or simply add to your existing meals. Sometimes changing to a new diet can be as dramatic as requiring you to clear out your entire kitchen cabinet and buying new ingredients, or it can be as simple as just buying one or two ingredients.

The Ketogenic or "Keto" diet is a diet that has been slowly gaining momentum over the last few years. It is a high-fat diet that is low in carbohydrates and moderates in protein.

It provides an almost perfect macro-nutrient ratio which makes it easy for the body to switch effortlessly from using fat to using carbohydrates.

The human body is highly dependent on both fat and carbohydrates for energy to fuel it throughout the day. What's fascinating about the Keto diet is that it can encourage the body to burn fat more rapidly. Scientists have for many years have noted that fat is solely responsible for weight gain, and weight gain is associated with multiple illnesses like obesity, Diabetes, and Epilepsy in children.

Not only are the ingredients important, but so too is the method in which you use to prepare your foods.

There are many kitchen appliances that can make this process a heck of a lot easier. With each passing day, air fryers are becoming more popular for the wonders they can create. You can make all your favorite dishes in an absolutely healthy way with air fryers. Are you intrigued? An air fryer is a must-have kitchen appliance that will ensure food is cooked through the circulation of hot air within the chamber. There is a mechanical fan present in the air fryer that circulates this hot air at high speed around the food. Instead of using gallons of oil, an air fryer needs only a few drops. In this book, more will be explored on the Keto diet using the wonderful air fryer. Enjoy the journey.

Introduction

Of all the diets, the Ketogenic diet is perhaps one of the trendiest these days. In order to lose fat and live healthily, it's necessary to cut down on carbohydrates. Our society is used to eating cereals, sugar, and products made with flour daily. Carbohydrates are normally the highest macronutrient that we consume in our food. Many studies show that carbohydrates are highly addictive, and are a main source of obesity. Carbohydrates are the main components of most of the delicious foods we are used to, and an ingredient heavily present on a lot of the ready-to-eat foods sold in grocery stores. In other words, it's just easy to eat carbs in our world.

In this book, we'll introduce you to the Ketogenic Diet and present a comprehensive list of recipes that you'll certainly be delighted to try while dieting.

When we say that you're going to cut down carbs, the first question that comes to mind is: "What am I going to eat?" For many people, the Ketogenic Diet is a fancy way of saying "eggs and bacon." However, our intention is to demystify and show you that the ketogenic diet can be as pleasant as a normal diet, and maybe even better.

There are plenty of communities formed around the Ketogenic diet on the web.

It is good to find these web communities to see the results of other people that have been through the Ketogenic diet and the positive results that the diet has helped achieve. This will be great motivation for whoever is beginning this exciting culinary journey. I'm excited to begin. Let's get started!

Keto Explained

The ketogenic diet causes ketone bodies to be produced by your liver, thus shifting your body's metabolism away from using glucose as the primary source of fuel and toward fat utilization. To accomplish this, the ketogenic diet restricts carbohydrate intake below a certain level – usually 100 grams per day. The daily amount depends on your health and weight loss goals.

How Does the Ketogenic Diet Work?

We all know that we need food for energy. On a typical high-carb diet, your body specifically uses glucose as the primary source of energy; it is easier for your body to convert carbs to glucose than it is with other types of energy sources.

Insulin will also be produced to process the glucose in your bloodstream, and the fats will get stored by the body, eventually piling up and causing a litany of health problems.

The ketogenic diet enables your body to use another energy source for fuel; the concept is that with a lower carb intake, you will be depriving your body of the glucose it needs and will make use of the fats instead, as it falls into a state known as ketosis.

Ketosis is a natural state of the body wherein the liver will break down the available fats instead of glucose or carbohydrates, and ketones will be produced which will then be burned by the body as the primary energy source, Your goal with the ketogenic diet is to force your body into this metabolic state.

Your body is designed to adapt to a metabolic state easily, so you only need to worry about following the diet and let your body handle the rest.

The ketogenic diet is different from other low-carb diets. The difference is that your diet should be about 70-75 percent of calories from fat, 20-25 percent from protein, and 5-10 percent from carbohydrates each day.

If you follow these guidelines, your diet will be composed of high-fats and moderate protein intake, and there will be no need to count calories

Protein is limited because it affects the insulin and blood sugar in your body.

If you consume protein in large quantities, the excess gets converted to glucose. As a result, your body will not reach a state of ketosis

Have you ever come to note that whenever you have a food craving, you usually go for carb-rich foods?

That's because your brain has labeled the starchy and sweet foods as comfort foods.

Our main goal with the ketogenic diet is to drastically reduce the intake of carbohydrates and choose a healthier alternative. In theory, if you limit your carb intake and achieve a state of ketosis, the excess weight will be shed easily.

How to know when you are in Ketosis

Whether you have taken any tests to discover your ketosis status, your body will exhibit physical signs to prompt you. You may have a loss of appetite, increased thirst, have bad breath, or notice a stronger urine smell. These are all clues from your body.

Ketosis and Your Sleep Patterns

After you have a good night of sleep, your body is in ketosis since you have been in a fasted state for 8 hours or more, you are on the way to burning ketones. If you are new to the high-fat and low-carb dieting, the optimal fat-burning state takes time. Your body has depended on bringing in carbs and glucose; it will not readily give up carbs and start to crave saturated fats.

The restless night is also a normal side effect. Vitamin supplements can sometimes remedy the problem that can be caused by a lowered insulin and serotonin level. For a quick fix; try one-half of a tablespoon of fruit spread and a square of chocolate.

Bad Breath Happens

You may notice a metallic or fruity taste with an odor similar to nail polish remover. This is the by-product of acetoacetic acid (acetone) that is an obvious indication. You may also experience a drier mouth. These changes are normal as a side effect as your body processes these high-fat foods.

Once you are accustomed to the Ketogenic dieting techniques, the bad breath symptoms will pass. If you are socializing, try a diet soda or a no-sugar drink.

Sugar-free gum is also a quick fix. Always check the nutrition labels for carbohydrate facts; you may be surprised. These are not allowed on the Keto diet because they reduce ketones. Therefore, only use it temporarily. If you are at home, just grab the toothbrush.

Lowered Appetite

When you reduce your carbs and proteins, you will be increasing your fat intake. The reduced appetite comes from the multitude of fibrous veggies, fats, and satiating nutrients provided in the new diet.

The "full" factor is a huge benefit to the Ketogenic plan. It will give you one less thing to worry about—being hungry.

Thirst is increased

Fluid retention is increased when you are consuming carbohydrates. Once the carbs are flushed away, water weight is lost. You counterbalance by increasing the water intake since you are probably dehydrated.

The Keto diet calls for one to have more water intake because you are storing carbs. If you are dehydrated, your body can use the stored carbs to restore hydration. When you're in ketosis, the carbs are removed, and your body doesn't have the water reserves. If you have tried other diets, you might have been dehydrated, but the higher carbohydrate counts stopped you from being thirsty.

Thus, the Keto state is a diuretic state, so drink plenty of water daily.

Digestive Issues

With the sudden change in diet; it's expected you may have problems including constipation or diarrhea when you first start the Keto diet. Individuals are different, and variation may rely on the foods you decide to eat to increase your fiber intake using various vegetables.

You may experience issues because your fiber intake may be too high in comparison to your previous diet. Try reducing certain "new" foods until the transitional phase of Keto is concluded. It should clear up with time.

You may be lacking beneficial bacteria. Try consuming fermented foods to increase your probiotics and aid digestion. You can benefit from B vitamins, omega-3 fatty acids, and beneficial enzymes as well.

Other Possible Side Effects

Induction Flu: The diet can make you irritable, nauseous, a bit confused, lethargic, and possibly suffer from a headache. Several days into the plan should remedy these effects. If not, add one-half of a teaspoon of salt to a glass of water and drink it to help with the side effects. You may need to do this once a day for about the first week, and it could take about 15 to 20 minutes before it helps. It will go away!

Constipation: During the Ketogenic plan you must drink plenty of water, or you could easily become constipated because of dehydration.

The low carbs contribute to the issue. Eat the right veggies and add a small amount of salt to your food to help with the movements. If all else fails, try some *Milk of Magnesia.*

Leg Cramps: The loss of magnesium (a mineral) can be a demon and create a bit of pain with the onset of the Keto diet plan changes. With the loss of the minerals during urination, you could experience bouts of cramps in your legs.

Heart Palpitations: You may begin to feel "fluttery" as a result of dehydration or because of an insufficient intake of salt. Try to make adjustments, but if you don't feel better quickly, you should seek emergency care.

The Health Benefits of the Ketogenic Diet

1. *Faster & sustainable weight loss*

Cutting carbs is the fastest and surest way to lose weight quickly. First, a low-carb diet, such as the Ketogenic diet, gets rid of all the excess water from your body. You will notice that there is a loss of water weight.

Additionally, since the Keto diet lowers your insulin levels, your kidneys start shedding the excess sodium which leads to rapid weight loss within the first two weeks

For as long as you remain committed to the Ketogenic diet, you will continue losing weight until you achieved your ideal weight

2. *Slimmer waistlines*

Not all the fat in your body is the same. Where the fat is stored in your body is what will determine how your weight affects your health. There is subcutaneous fat which is stored under the skin and visceral fat that is stored within your abdominal cavity

Visceral fat is dangerous because it tends to lodge around your organs. Fat around your abdomen can fuel insulin resistance and inflammation and is believed to be the leading cause of chronic illnesses

The Ketogenic diet is very effective at reducing visceral fat, and you will notice your waistline shrinking when you start following the Ketogenic diet

3. *Increased levels of good cholesterol*

Good cholesterol is biologically referred to as High-Density Lipoprotein (HDL). Good cholesterol levels tend to increase under the Ketogenic diet as your body carried the Low-Density Lipoprotein (LDL) or the bad cholesterol away from your body and into the liver where it is recycled and excreted as waste

4. *Kills Your Appetite.*

Hunger and deprivation are the worst side effects of any diet, and this is one of the main reasons why most diets fail. But not the Keto diet.

By cutting carbs and replacing them with healthy fats and protein, your body will take more time to digest fats and proteins than it did carbs and you will naturally eat less. In the end, you'll stay full longer and lose more weight!

5. Reduced symptoms of type 2 diabetes

When you eat a lot of carbs, your body breaks them down into simple sugars. Once this glucose gets into your bloodstream, it elevates your blood sugar levels and triggers the release of insulin. The release of insulin instructs your cells to take in the glucose and use it, or store it as fat for later use,

Continued intake of low-quality carbs, such as white bread or sweetened beverages, can lead to insulin resistance. When this happens, your cells are not able to recognize insulin, and it becomes harder for your body to take the blood sugar into your cells. This is what leads to type 2 diabetes

Reversing this cycle requires one to cut carbs from their diet to the point where the body doesn't need to release high amounts of insulin.

Air Fryer and How It Works?

Air Fryer is a kitchen appliance with versatility and ingenious design, with patented technology that cooks food by super-heated air. It heats up within a minute, and there is a swift flow of hot air within the dedicated chamber making food to cook evenly while using less oil.

This game-changing kitchen appliance has the rapid air circulation technology which enables hot air to surround the food you want to cook at high speeds to develop the crispy food we all crave for. On top of the delicious crunchy food, little oil is used in the process which makes it a guilt-free delicacy!

Tips to Prepare Healthy Foods in Air Fryer

1. Vegetables are one of the easiest foods to cook in Air Fryer. A wide variety of plants can be cooked, be it delicate beans to root vegetables. For the best cooking experience, firstly, soak the vegetables, especially the harder ones, in cold water for 15 - 20 minutes. Then after, dry them using a clean kitchen towel.

2. Roasting with air is a new cooking trend you have to try because you can finally prepare your winter favorites

3. Flip foods when half the cooking time is attained; Just as you would if you were cooking on a grill or in a skillet, you need to turn foods over so that they brown evenly.

4. You can bake your favorite recipes in your Air Fryer but always check with the machine's manual before using new baking ware with Air Fryer

5. Aim at cooking your food to the desired doneness because the recipes are flexible and they are designed for all Air Fryer models.

If you feel that the food needs more cooking time, then adjust it and cook for a few more minutes. It is not necessary to stick to a recipe time, as certain ingredients can vary in their size and firmness from one place to another

6. When it comes to cooking time, it changes depending on the particular Air Fryer model, the size of food, food pre-preparation and so on. For shorter cooking cycles, you should preheat Air Fryer for about 3 - 4 minutes. otherwise, if you put the ingredients into the cold cooking basket, the cooking time needs to be increased to 3 additional minutes.

7. Use a good quality oil spray to brush food and cooking basket; it is also helpful for easy cleanup

Breakfast Recipes

Delicious Breakfast Soufflé

Servings: 4

Ingredients:

- 6 eggs
- 1/3 c. milk
- ½ c. mozzarella cheese, shredded
- 1 tbsp. chopped parsley
- ½ c. ham, chopped
- 1 tsp. salt
- 1 tsp. black pepper
- ½ tsp. garlic powder

Directions:

1. Grease 4 ramekins with a nonstick cooking spray.
2. Preheat your air fryer to 350 degrees Fahrenheit.
3. Using a large bowl, add and stir all the ingredients until it mixes properly.
4. Pour the egg mixture into the greased ramekins and place it inside your air fryer.
5. Cook it inside your air fryer for 8 minutes.
6. Then carefully remove the souffle from your air fryer and allow it to cool off.
7. Serve and enjoy!

Nutritional Information:

Calories: 195, Fat: 15g, Protein: 9g, Carbs: 6g,

Yummy Breakfast Italian Frittata

Servings: 4

Ingredients:

- 6 eggs
- 1/3 c. milk
- 4 oz. Italian sausage, chopped
- 3 c. chopped kale
- 1 red bell pepper, deseeded and chopped
- ½ c. grated feta cheese
- 1 zucchini, chopped
- 1 tbsp. basil, chopped
- 1 tsp. garlic powder
- 1 tsp. onion powder
- 1 sp. salt
- 1 tsp. black pepper

Directions:

1. Preheat your air fryer to 360 degrees Fahrenheit.
2. Grease the air fryer pan with a nonstick cooking spray.
3. To the pan, add Italian sausage and cook it inside your air fryer for 5 minutes.
4. While doing that, add and stir in the remaining ingredients until it mixes properly.
5. Combine the egg mixture to the pan and allow it to cook inside your air fryer for 5 minutes.
6. Thereafter carefully remove the pan and allow it to cool off until it gets chilly enough to serve.
7. Serve and enjoy!

Nutritional Information:

Calories: 225, Fat: 14g, Protein: 20g, Carbs: 4.5g

Savory Cheese and Bacon Muffins

Servings: 4

Ingredients:

- 1 ½ c. all-purpose flour
- 2 tsps. baking powder
- ½ c. milk
- 2 eggs
- 1 tbsp. parsley, chopped
- 4 chopped bacon slices cooked
- onion, chopped
- ½ c. cheddar cheese, shredded
- ½ tsp. onion powder
- 1 tsp. salt
- 1 tsp. black pepper

Directions:

1. Preheat your air fryer to 360 degrees Fahrenheit.
2. Using a large bowl, add and stir all the ingredients until it mixes properly.
3. Then grease the muffin cups with a nonstick cooking spray or line it with a parchment paper. Pour the batter proportionally into each muffin cup.
4. Place it inside your air fryer and bake it for 15 minutes.
5. Thereafter, carefully remove it from your air fryer and allow it to chill.
6. Serve and enjoy!

Nutritional Information:

Calories: 180, Fat: 18g, Protein: 15g, Carbs: 16g

Best Air-Fried English Breakfast

Servings: 4

Ingredients:

- sausages
- bacon slices
- 4 eggs
- 16 oz. baked beans
- slices of toast

Directions:

1 Add the sausages and bacon slices to your air fryer and cook them for 10 minutes at a 320 degrees Fahrenheit.

2 Using a ramekin or heat-safe bowl, add the baked beans, then place another ramekin and add the eggs and whisk.

3 Increase the temperature to 290 degrees Fahrenheit.

4 Place it inside your air fryer and cook it for an additional 10 minutes or until everything is done.

5 Serve and enjoy!

Nutritional Information:

Calories: 850, Fat: 40g, Protein: 48g, Carbs: 20g

Air Bread & Egg Butter

Servings: 19

Ingredients:

- 3 eggs
- 1 tsp. baking powder
- ¼ tsp. sea salt
- 1 c. almond flour
- ¼ c. butter

Directions:

1 Soften the butter to room temperature. Whisk the eggs with a hand mixer. Combine the two and add the rest of the fixings to make a dough.
2 Knead the dough and cover with a tea towel for about 10 minutes.
3 Set the Air Fryer at 350°F.
4 Air fry the bread for 15 minutes.
5 Remove the bread and let it cool down on a wooden board.
6 Slice and serve with your favorite meal or as it is.

Nutritional Information:

Calories: 40, Fat: 3.9g, Protein: 1.2g, Carbs: 0.5g

Egg Butter

Servings: 4

Ingredients:

- 4 eggs
- 1 tsp. salt
- 4 tbsps. butter

Directions:

1 Add a layer of foil to the Air Fryer basket and add the eggs. Cook at 320°F for 17 minutes. Transfer to an ice-cold water bath to chill.

2 Peel and chop the eggs and combine with the rest of the fixings. Combine well until it achieves a creamy texture.

3 Enjoy with your Air Fried Bread. Doesn't that sound heavenly?

Nutritional Information:

Calories: 164, Fat: 8.5g, Protein: 3g, Carbs: 2.67g

Avocado Egg Boats

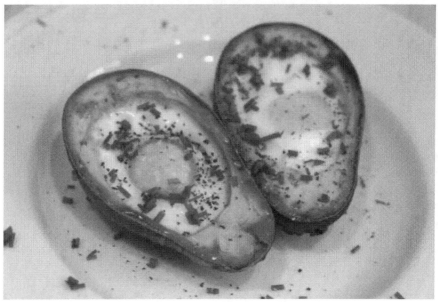

Servings: 2

Ingredients:

- 1 avocado
- 2 eggs
- Chopped chives
- Chopped parsley
- Pepper
- Salt

Directions:

1. Warm up the fryer to 350°F.
2. Remove the pit from the avocado. Slice and scoop out part of the flesh. Shake with the seasonings.
3. Add an egg to each half and place in the preheated Air Fryer for 6 minutes.
4. Remove and serve with some additional parsley and chives if desired.

Nutritional Information:

Calories: 288, Fat: 26g, Protein: 7.6g, Carbs: 9.4 g

Avocado Muffins

Servings: 7

Ingredients:

- 1 c. almond flour
- ½ tsp. baking soda
- 1 tsp. apple cider vinegar
- 1 egg
- 4 tbsps. butter
- 3 scoops stevia powder
- ½ c. pitted avocado
- 1 oz. melted dark chocolate

Directions:

1. Preheat the Air Fryer to 355°F.
2. Whisk the almond flour, baking soda, and vinegar. Add the stevia powder and melted chocolate.
3. Whisk the egg in another container and add to the mixture along with the butter.
4. Peel, cube, and mash the avocado and add. Blend with a hand mixer to make the flour mixture smooth. Pour into the muffin forms (½ full). Cook for 9 minutes.
5. Lower the heat (340°F) and cook for 3 more minutes.
6. Chill before serving for the best results.

Nutritional Information:

Calories: 133, Fat: 12.4g, Protein: 2.2g, Carbs: 2.9g

Bacon & Cheese Muffins

Servings: 6

Ingredients:

- 1 large egg
- 4 large slices of bacon
- 1 medium. diced onion
- 2 tbsps. olive oil
- 2 tsps. baking powder
- 1 c. Milk
- 1 c. Shredded cheddar cheese
- 1½ c. almond flour
- 1 tsp. parsley
- Pepper
- Salt
- 6 muffin tins to fit in the basket

Directions:

1. Set the temperature on the Air Fryer to 356°F.
2. Prepare the bacon slices with a small amount of oil. Add the onion when it's about ¾ ready. Sauté and set aside when translucent. Drain on towels.
3. Mix the rest of the fixings and stir well. Add the onions and bacon.
4. Stir well and add the batter into 6 muffin holders. Add to the fryer basket for 20 minutes. Lower the heat for 10 minutes (320°F).
5. Serve and enjoy right out of the fryer.

Nutritional Information:

Calories: 251, Fat: 20g, Protein: 12g, Carbs: 6g

Chicken Hash

Servings: 3

Ingredients:

- 7 oz. chicken fillet
- 6 oz. chopped cauliflower
- ½ yellow diced onion
- 1 chopped green pepper
- 1 tbsp. Water
- 1 tbsp. Cream
- 1 tsp. black pepper
- 3 tbsps. butter

Directions:

1. Program the Air Fryer to 380°F. Chop the cauliflower and add to a blender to make rice. Chop the chicken into bite-sized pieces and sprinkle with salt and pepper.
2. Prepare the veggies and combine the fixings.
3. Add the fryer basket and cook until done (6-7 minutes). Watch closely to prevent scorching.
4. Serve and enjoy.

Nutritional Information:

Calories: 261, Fat: 16.2g, Protein: 21g, Carbs: 7.1g

Chicken Strips

Servings: 4

Ingredients:

- 1 lb. chicken fillets
- 1 t. paprika
- 1 tbsp. cream
- ½ t. salt & pepper

Directions:

1. Dice the fillets into strips. Season to your liking with the salt and pepper.
2. Set the Air Fryer at 365°F and add the butter to the basket.
3. Arrange the strips in the basket and air fry for 6 minutes.
4. Flip the strips and cook for another 5 minutes.
5. When done, sprinkle with the cream and paprika. Serve warm.

Nutritional Information:

Calories: 245, Fat: 11.5g, Protein: 33g, Carbs: 0.6g

Delicious Eggs, Ham, & Spinach

Servings: 4

Ingredients:

- 7 oz. sliced ham
- 2¼ c. spinach
- 4 tsps. cream milk
- 1 tbsp. olive oil
- 4 large eggs
- Salt
- Pepper
- 4 ramekins
- Cooking spray
- 1 Skillet

Directions:

1. Set the fryer temperature to 356°F. Spray the ramekins.
2. Warm up the oil in a skillet (medium heat) and sauté the spinach until wilted. Drain.
3. Divide the spinach and rest of the fixings in each of the ramekins.
4. Sprinkle with the salt and pepper. Bake until set (20 minutes).
5. Serve when they are to your liking.

Nutritional Information:

Calories: 190, Fat: 13g, Protein: 15g, Carbs: 3g

Egg Pizza

Servings: 1

Ingredients:

- 2 eggs
- ½ t. of each:
- Dried oregano
- Dried basil
- 2 tbsps. shredded mozzarella cheese
- 4 thin slices of pepperoni
- 1 ramekin

Directions:

1. Whisk the eggs with the oregano and basil.
2. Pour into the ramekin and top off with the pepperoni and cheese.
3. Arrange the ramekin in the air fryer. Prepare for 3 minutes and serve.

Nutritional Information:

Calories: 285, Fat: 18g, Protein: 22g, Carbs: 8g

Eggs in a Zucchini Nest

Servings: 4

Ingredients:

- 8 oz. grated zucchini
- 4 t. butter
- ¼ tsp. sea salt
- ½ tsp. Black pepper
- ½ tsp. Paprika
- 4 eggs
- 4 oz. shredded cheddar cheese
- 4 ramekins

Directions:

1. Preheat the Air Fryer at 356ºF.
2. Grate the zucchini. Add the butter to the ramekins and add the zucchini in a nest shape. Sprinkle with the paprika, salt, and pepper.
3. Whisk the eggs and add to the nest, topping it off with the cheese.
4. Air fry for 7 minutes. Chill for 3 minutes and serve in the ramekin.

Nutritional Information:

Calories: 221, Fat: 17.7g, Protein: 13.4g, Carbs: 2.9g

Mushroom, Onion, & Cheese Frittata

Servings: 2

Ingredients:

- 1 tbsp. olive oil
- 2 c. sliced mushrooms
- 1 small sliced onion
- 3 eggs
- ½ c. grated cheese
- Salt
- 1 Skillet

Directions:

1. Program the Air Fryer to 320°F.
2. Warm up a skillet (medium heat) and add the oil.
3. Toss in the mushrooms and onions and sauté for about 5 minutes. Add to the Air Fryer.
4. Whisk the eggs with the salt and dump on top of the fixings in the fryer.
5. Sprinkle with the cheese and air fry for 10 minutes.
6. Take right out of the basket and serve. Yummy!

Nutritional Information:

Calories: 284, Fat: 22g, Protein: 17g, Carbs: 6g

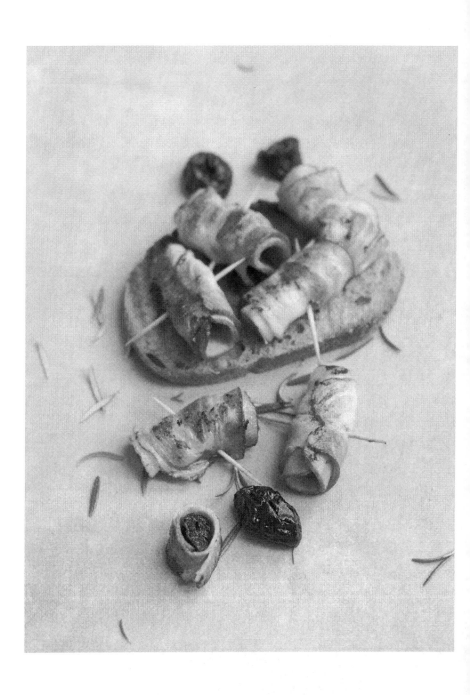

Beef

Beef Rib Steak with Parsley Lemon Butter

Servings: 4

Ingredients:

- 2 beef rib eye steak
- 2 tbsps. extra virgin olive oil
- ¼ tsp. salt
- ½ tsp. pepper
- ½ c. butter
- ¼ c. chopped fresh parsley
- 2 cloves garlic
- ¼ tsp. grated lemon zest
- 2 tbsps. lemon juice
- 1 tsp. basil
- ¼ tsp. cayenne

Directions:

1. Brush the beef rib eye steak with olive oil then sprinkle salt and pepper over the beef. Let it sit for about 30 minutes.
2. Meanwhile, place butter in a bowl then pours lemon juice over the butter.
3. Using a fork mix until the butter is smooth.
4. Grate the garlic then add to the butter.
5. Stir in chopped fresh parsley, grated lemon zest, basil, and cayenne to the butter then mix well. Store in the fridge.
6. Preheat an Air Fryer to 400°F (204°C) and put a rack in the Air Fryer.
7. Place the seasoned beef rib eye on the rack then set the time to 15 minutes. Cook the beef.
8. Once the beef rib eye is ready, remove from the Air Fryer then place on a serving dish.
9. Serve with the butter sauce.
10. Enjoy right away!

Nutritional Information:

Calories: 432, Fat: 42.7g, Protein: 10.6g, Carbs: 4.1g

Marinated Flank Steak with Beef Gravy

Servings: 2

Ingredients:

- 1 flank steak
- ¼ c. butter
- 3½ tbsps. Lemon juice
- 4 tbsps. Minced garlic
- ½ tsp. salt
- ½ tsp. pepper
- 1 c. chopped onion
- ¼ c. beef broth
- 2 tbsps. coconut milk
- 3 tbsps. coconut aminos
- 1 tsp. nutmeg
- 1 scoop Stevia
- 1 tbsp. extra virgin olive oil

Directions:

1. Allow the butter to melt in the microwave then let it cool.
2. Combine the melted butter with lemon juice, minced garlic, salt, and pepper then mix well.
3. Season the flank steak with the spice mixture then marinate for at least 3 hours. Store in the refrigerator to keep it fresh.
4. Preheat a saucepan over medium heat then pour olive oil into the saucepan.
5. Once the oil is hot, stir in chopped onion then sauté until translucent and aromatic.
6. Pour beef broth into the saucepan then season with nutmeg. Bring to boil.
7. Once it is boiled, reduce the heat then add coconut milk, coconut aminos, and stevia to the saucepan. Stir until dissolved.
8. Get the sauce off heat then let it cool.
9. After 3 hours, remove the seasoned flank steak from the refrigerator then thaw at room temperature.
10. Preheat an Air Fryer to 400°F (204°C).
11. Once the Air Fryer is ready, place the seasoned flank steak in the Air Fryer then set the time to 15 minutes.
12. After 15 minutes, open the Air Fryer then drizzle the beef gravy over the flank steak.

13. Cook the flank steak again and set the time to 5 minutes.
14. Remove the cooked flank steak from the Air Fryer then place on a serving dish.
15. Drizzle the gravy on top then enjoy right away.

Nutritional Information:

Calories: 432, Fat: 42.7g, Protein: 10.6g, Carbs: 4.1g

Buttery Beef Loin and Cheese Sauce

Servings: 3

Ingredients:

- 1 lb. beef loin
- 1 tbsp. butter
- 1 tbsp. minced garlic
- ½ tsp. salt
- ½ tsp. dried parsley
- ¼ tsp. thyme
- ½ c. sour cream
- ¾ c. cream cheese
- 2 tbsps. grated cheddar cheese
- ¼ tsp. pepper
- ¼ tsp. nutmeg

Directions:

1. Place butter in a microwave-safe bowl then melts the butter.
2. Combine with minced garlic, salt, dried parsley, and thyme then mix well.
3. Cut the beef loin into slices then brush with the butter mixture.
4. Preheat an Air Fryer to 400°F (204°C).
5. Once the Air Fryer is ready, place the seasoned beef loin in the Air Fryer and set the time to 15 minutes. Cook the beef loin.
6. Meanwhile, place cream cheese in a mixing bowl then using an electric mixer beat until smooth and fluffy.
7. Add sour cream, and grated cheese then seasons with pepper and nutmeg. Beat again until fluffy then store in the fridge.
8. Once the beef loin is done, remove from the Air Fryer then place on a serving dish.
9. Serve and enjoy with cheese sauce.

Nutritional Information:

Calories: 441, Fat: 39.4g, Protein: 15.7g, Carbs: 5.6g

Servings: 4

Ingredients:

- ½ beef ribs
- 1 tbsps. lemon juice
- 1 egg
- 3 tbsps. coconut milk
- 1 c. roasted pecans
- 1 tsp. ginger
- ¼ tsp. cayenne
- ¼ tsp. salt
- ½ tsp. pepper
- 1 tbsp. extra virgin olive oil

Directions:

1. Splash lemon juice over the beef ribs then let it rest for a few minutes.
2. Meanwhile, crack the egg then pour coconut milk into the egg. Stir until incorporated.
3. Place roasted pecans in a food processor then season with ginger, cayenne, salt, and pepper. Process until becoming flour texture.
4. Dip the beef ribs in the egg mixture then roll into the pecan mixture. Make sure the rib is completely coated with the pecans.
5. Preheat an Air Fryer to 400°F (204°C) and put a rack in the Air Fryer.
6. Once the Air Fryer is ready, place the coated beef ribs on the rack.
7. Spray olive oil over the beef ribs then cook the beef ribs. Set the time to 15 minutes.
8. Once it is done, remove from the Air Fryer and serve warm.
9. Enjoy!

Nutritional Information:

Calories: 396, Fat: 38g, Protein: 12.4g, Carbs: 5.2g

Beef Meatloaf Tomato

Servings: 8s

Ingredients:

- 2 c. ground beef
- 1 egg
- ½ c. tomato puree
- ½ tsp. salt
- ¾ tsp. pepper
- 1 c. cheddar cheese cubes
- ¼ c. chopped onion
- 3 tbsps. minced garlic

Directions:

1. Crash the eggs then place in a bowl.
2. Season with salt, pepper, and minced garlic then whisk until incorporated.
3. Pour the egg mixture into the ground beef then mix well.
4. Add cheese cubes, and chopped onion to the mixture then mix until combined.
5. Transfer the beef mixture to a silicon loaf pan then spread evenly.
6. Drizzle tomato puree on top then set aside.
7. Preheat an Air Fryer to 350°F (177°C).
8. Place the silicon loaf pan on the Air Fryer rack then cook the meatloaf for 20 minutes.
9. Once it is done, remove from the Air Fryer then let it cool.
10. Cut the beef meatloaf into slices then serve.
11. Enjoy!

Nutritional Information:

Calories: 242, Fat: 19.3g, Protein: 13.7g, Carbs: 3.1g

Minty Beef Balls with Lemon Yogurt Dip

Servings: 8

Ingredients:

- 1 lb. ground beef
- ¼ tsp. salt
- ¼ tsp. pepper
- ¾ tsp. cumin
- ¾ tsp. coriander
- ¾ tsp. cayenne pepper
- 2 tsps. minced garlic
- 1 tbsp. chopped mint leaves
- 1 tbsp. chopped parsley
- 1 egg
- ½ c. grated coconut
- ¾ c. Greek yogurt
- ¼ c. sour cream
- 2 tbsps. lemon juice
- ½ tsp. grated lemon zest

Directions:

1. Combine ground beef with cumin, coriander, cayenne pepper, minced garlic, chopped mint leaves, and chopped parsley in a dish.
2. Season using pepper and salt then combine well.
3. Shape the beef mixture into small balls then set aside.
4. Crack the eggs then stir until incorporated.
5. Place the balls in the beaten egg then roll in the grated coconut.
6. Preheat an Air Fryer to 375°F (191°C).
7. Arrange the balls in the preheated Air Fryer then cook for 7 minutes.
8. While waiting for the beef balls, place Greek yogurt, sour cream, lemon juice, and lemon zest in a mixing bowl.
9. Beat the mixture until smooth and fluffy with an electric mixer. Store in the refrigerator.
10. Once the beef balls are done remove from the Air Fryer, then place on a serving dish.
11. Drizzle lemon yogurt over the beef balls then serve.
12. Enjoy!

Nutritional Information:

Calories: 230, Fat: 18.2g, Protein: 13.1g, Carbs: 2.2g

Cheesy Beef Empanadas

Servings: 6

Ingredients:

- 2 c. Mozzarella cheese
- 1 c. cream cheese
- 1½ c. almond flour
- 2 eggs
- 2½ c. ground beef
- ¼ c. butter
- ½ c. chopped onion
- ¼ tsp. salt
- ½ tsp. black pepper
- ½ tsp. nutmeg

Directions:

1. Place butter in a microwave-safe bowl then melts the butter.
2. Pour the melted butter over the beef then add chopped onion to the bowl.
3. Season with salt, black pepper, and nutmeg then stir well.
4. Preheat an Air Fryer to 400°F (204°C).
5. Transfer the seasoned beef to the Air Fryer then cook for 10 minutes.
6. Remove the beef from the Air Fryer then let it cool.
7. Next, place grated Mozzarella cheese and cream cheese in a microwave-safe bowl then melt the mixture.
8. Once the cheese is melted, add eggs to the bowl then stir until incorporated.
9. Stir in almond flour to the cheese mixture then mix until becoming a soft dough.
10. Place the dough on a flat surface then roll until thin.
11. Using a circle cookies mold cut the thin dough into 12.
12. Put about 2 tbsp.s of beef on a circle dough then fold until becoming a half-circle. Glue with water.
13. Repeat with the remaining dough and beef then set aside.

14. Preheat an Air Fryer to 425°F (218°C).
15. Arrange the beef empanadas in the Air Fryer then cook for 12 minutes or until lightly golden brown.
16. Remove from the Air Fryer then serve warm. Enjoy!

Nutritional Information:

Calories: 283, Fat: 26.8g, Protein: 8.7g, Carbs: 3.6g

Cheesy Melt Beef Bombs

Servings: 4

Ingredients:

- 1 lb. ground beef
- 1 c. chopped onion
- ¼ tsp. salt
- ½ tsp. pepper
- 3 egg yolks
- 1 c. grated Mozzarella cheese
- 1 tbsp. extra virgin olive oil

Directions:

1. Put the ground beef, and chopped onion in a bowl then season with salt and pepper.
2. Add egg yolks to the beef mixture then mix until combined.
3. Shape the ground beef mixture into small or medium balls and fill each beef ball with grated Mozzarella cheese.
4. Preheat an Air Fryer to 375°F (191°C).
5. Place the beef balls in the Air Fryer then spray with olive oil.
6. Set the time to 10 minutes and cook the beef balls.
7. Once it is done, remove the beef balls from the Air Fryer then serve.

Nutritional Information:

Calories: 436, Fat: 36.2g, Protein: 22.5g, Carbs: 4.3g

Jalapeno Spicy Fried Beef

Servings: 8

Ingredients:

- 1 beef roast
- 2 jalapenos
- 2 tbsps. coconut oil
- ¼ tsp. salt
- ½ tsp. black pepper
- 2 tbsps. lemon juice
- 3 tbsps. minced garlic
- ½ c. chopped onion
- 1 c. sliced bell pepper
- ½ c. butter
- 1 tsp. cayenne
- 1 tbsp. red chili flakes
- 1 tbsp. hot sauce
- 1 tbsp. dried parsley

Directions:

1. Cut the jalapenos into small pieces then combine with salt, black pepper, lemon juice, and minced garlic.
2. Season the beef roast with the spice mixture then let it rest for a few minutes.
3. Preheat an Air Fryer to 400°F (204°C).
4. Once the Air Fryer is ready, place the seasoned beef roast in the Air Fryer then spray with coconut oil.
5. Sprinkle chopped onion and sliced bell pepper on over the beef roast then cook for 18 minutes.
6. Meanwhile, melt butter in a saucepan then remove from heat.
7. Add cayenne, red chili flakes, hot sauce, and dried parsley then stir until combined.
8. Once the beef roast is done, drizzle the butter sauce over the beef roast then cook for another 20 minutes.
9. Transfer the cooked beef roast to a serving dish then enjoy.

Nutritional Information:

Calories: 444, Fat: 35.3g, Protein: 25.4g, Carbs: 7g

Rosemary Rib Eye Beef Steak

Servings: 2

Ingredients:

- 2 rib eye beefsteak
- ¼ c. chopped rosemary
- 2 tsps. minced garlic
- ¼ c. butter
- 1½ tbsps. balsamic vinegar
- ½ tsp. salt
- ½ tsp. black pepper

Directions:

1. Set Allow the butter to melt in a saucepan over low heat then add minced garlic to the saucepan. Sauté until aromatic.
2. Remove from heat then season with balsamic vinegar, salt, and pepper. Let it cool.
3. Add chopped rosemary to the mixture then stir well.
4. Place the rib eye in a zipper-lock plastic bag then add the spice mixture to the plastic bag.
5. Shake the plastic bag and make sure the rib eye is completely seasoned.
6. Marinate the rib eye for at least an hour and store in the fridge to keep it fresh.
7. After an hour, remove the seasoned ribeye from the fridge then thaw at room temperature.
8. Preheat an Air Fryer to 400°F (204°C) and place a rack in it.
9. Once the Air Fryer is preheated, place the seasoned ribeye n the rack then cook for 15 minutes.
10. Once it is done, remove from the Air Fryer then transfer to a serving dish.
11. Serve and enjoy.

Nutritional Information:

Calories: 544, Fat: 49.2g, Protein: 20.8g, Carbs: 6g

Coffee-Chili Beef Ribs

Servings: 2

Ingredients:

- 1 rib eye
- ¼ c. espresso coffee
- ¼ c. chili powder
- 2½ tbsps. paprika
- 1½ tbsps. mustard
- ½ tsp. salt
- ¾ tsp. black pepper
- 1¼ tbsps. coriander
- ¾ tbsp. oregano
- 1½ tsps. ginger
- ¼ c. butter
- ¼ c. heavy cream
- ¼ c. strong coffee water

Directions:

1. Combine coffee powder with chili powder, paprika, mustard, coriander, oregano, and ginger in a bowl.
2. Add salt, and black pepper then mix well.
3. Rub the ribeye with the spice mixture then let it rest for at least 20 minutes.
4. After 20 minutes, preheat an Air Fryer to 400°F (204°C) and place a rack in the Air Fryer.
5. Once the Air Fryer is done, arrange the beef ribs on the rack then set the time to 8 minutes.
6. After 8 minutes, open the Air Fryer. Flip the beef and cook again for another 8 minutes.
7. Meanwhile, melt butter in a saucepan over low heat.
8. The moment your butter has melted, get off the heat and let it cool.
9. Add heavy cream, and coffee water to the melted butter then stir until incorporated. The sauce will be thickened.
10. Remove the cooked beef ribs from the Air Fryer then place on a serving dish.
11. Serve with coffee sauce then enjoy right away.

Nutritional Information:

Calories: 275, Fat: 21.6g, Protein: 14.3g, Carbs: 9.3g

Avocado Flank Steak with Cilantro

Servings: 2

Ingredients:

- 1 flank steak
- ½ tsp. salt
- ½ tsp. pepper
- 2 ripe avocados
- 1 c. chopped fresh cilantro
- 1½ tbsps. oregano
- 1 tsp. minced garlic
- 2 tbsps. butter
- 1 tbsp. lemon juice
- ½ tsp. red chili flakes

Directions:

1. Rub the flank steak with salt and pepper then let it sit for about 20 minutes.
2. Place butter in a microwave-safe bowl then melts the butter. Let it cool.
3. Meanwhile, place fresh cilantro in a food processor then season with oregano, minced garlic, and chili flakes.
4. Drizzle lemon juice over the cilantro then processes until smooth.
5. Cut the avocados into halves then discard the seeds.
6. Scoop out the avocado flesh then place in a bowl. Using a tablespoon, mash the avocados.
7. Add cilantro mixture to the mashed avocado then drizzle melted butter on top. Mix until combined then set aside.
8. Preheat an Air Fryer to 400°F (204°C) and put a rack in the Air Fryer.
9. Once the Air Fryer is ready, place the seasoned flank steak on the rack the cook for 6 minutes.
10. After 6 minutes, flip the flank steak and cook again for another 6 minutes.
11. Once it is done, remove from the Air Fryer then place on a serving dish.
12. Drizzle the cilantro and avocado mixture on top then serve.
13. Enjoy!

Nutritional Information:

Calories: 616, Fat: 55.6g, Protein: 16.1g, Carbs: 20.1g

Poultry

Chicken Wings Black Pepper with Sesame Seeds

Servings: 2

Ingredients:

- 2 lbs. chicken wings
- 1½ tsps. salt
- 1½ tsps. black pepper
- 1¼ tbsps. ginger powder
- 1½ tbsps. minced garlic
- 1½ tbsps. extra virgin olive oil
- ½ tbsp. mayonnaise
- 1 tbsp. sesame seeds

Directions:

1. Place salt, black pepper, ginger powder, and minced garlic in a bowl then mix well.
2. Rub the chicken wings with the spice mixture then let them sit for about 5 minutes.
3. Preheat an Air Fryer to 400°F (204°C).
4. Brush the chicken wings with extra virgin olive oil then arrange in the Air Fryer.
5. Cook the chicken wings for 15 minutes then arrange on a serving dish.
6. Drizzle mayonnaise over the chicken wings then sprinkles sesame seeds on top.
7. Serve and enjoy warm.

Nutritional Information:

Calories: 207, Fat: 16.9g, Protein: 7.1g, Carbs: 8g

Spicy Chicken Curry Samosa

Servings: 4

Ingredients:

- 1 lb. ground chicken
- 5 tbsps. extra virgin olive oil
- ¼ c. chopped onion
- ½ tsp. curry powder
- ¼ tsp. turmeric
- ¼ tsp. coriander
- 2 tsps. red chili flakes
- 2 tbsps. diced tomatoes
- ¾ c. almond flour
- ¼ c. water

Directions:

1. Place ground chicken, chopped onion, curry powder, turmeric, coriander, red chili flakes, and diced tomatoes in a bowl. Mix well.
2. Preheat an Air Fryer to 375°F (191°C) and spray a tbsp. of extra virgin olive in the Air Fryer.
3. Transfer the ground chicken mixture to the Air Fryer then cook for 10 minutes.
4. Once the chicken is cooked through, transfer from the Air Fryer to a container. Let it cool.
5. Meanwhile, combine almond flour with 3 tbsp.s of olive oil and water then mix until becoming dough.
6. Place the dough on a flat surface then roll until thin.
7. Using a 3-inches circle mold cookies cut the thin dough.
8. Put 2 tbsp.s of chicken on circle dough then fold it. Repeat with the remaining dough and chicken.
9. Preheat an Air Fryer to 400°F (204°C).
10. Brush each chicken samosa with the remaining virgin olive oil then arrange in the Air Fryer.
11. Cook the chicken samosas for 10 minutes then remove from the Air Fryer.
12. Arrange on a serving dish then serve with homemade tomato sauce or green cayenne.
13. Enjoy warm.

Nutritional Information:

Calories: 365, Fat: 30.3g, Protein: 23.1g, Carbs: 2.5g

Garlic Chicken Balls

Servings: 4

Ingredients:

- ½ lb. boneless chicken thighs
- ½ c. chopped mushroom
- 1 tsp. minced garlic
- 1 tsp. pepper
- ½ tsp. salt
- 1¼ c. roasted pecans
- 1 tsp. extra virgin olive oil

Directions:

1. Cut the boneless chicken into cubes then place in a food processor.
2. Add roasted pecans to the food processor then season with minced garlic, pepper, and salt. Process until smooth.
3. Cut the mushrooms into very small dices then add to the chicken mixture.
4. Using your hand mix the chicken with diced mushrooms then shape into small balls. Set aside.
5. Preheat an Air Fryer to 375°F (191°C).
6. Brush the balls with extra virgin olive oil then arrange the chicken balls in the Air Fryer.
7. Cook the chicken balls for 18 minutes then arrange on a serving dish.
8. Serve and enjoy.

Nutritional Information:

Calories: 525, Fat: 46.8g, Protein: 23.7g, Carbs: 5.7g

Servings: 4

Ingredients:

- 1½ lbs. chicken thighs
- 2 tsps. fennel
- 1 c. chopped onion
- ¾ tbsp. coconut oil
- 1½ tsp. ginger
- 2½ tsp. minced garlic
- 1½ tsp. smoked paprika
- 1 tsp. curry
- ½ tsp. turmeric
- ½ tsp. salt
- ½ tsp. pepper
- 1½ c. coconut milk

Directions:

1. Place fennel, chopped onion, and smoked paprika in a bowl.
2. Season with salt, minced garlic, ginger, curry, pepper, and turmeric then pour coconut oil into the mixture. Mix well.
3. Marinate the chicken thighs with the spice mixture then let them sit for 30 minutes.
4. After 30 minutes, preheat an Air Fryer to 375°F (191°C).
5. Transfer the chicken together with the spices to the Air Fryer then cook for 15 minutes.
6. After that, pour coconut milk over the chicken then stir well.
7. Cook the chicken again and set the time to 10 minutes.
8. Once it is done, arrange the chicken on a serving dish then pour the gravy over the chicken.
9. Enjoy!

Nutritional Information:

Calories: 414, Fat: 33.7g, Protein: 22.5g, Carbs: 6.4g

Gingery Chicken Satay

Servings: 8

Ingredients:

- 2 lbs. boneless chicken
- 2 tsps. minced garlic
- 1 tsp. ginger
- 2 tsps. sliced scallions
- 1 tsp. coriander
- 2 tbsps. coconut aminos
- ½ c. roasted cashews
- 1½ c. coconut milk

Directions:

1. Cut the chicken into cubes then rub with minced garlic, ginger, sliced scallions, and coriander. Let it sit for about 15 minutes.
2. Meanwhile, place roasted cashews in a blender then pour coconut milk into the blender.
3. Add coconut aminos to the blender then blend until smooth.
4. Pour the cashews, and coconut milk mixture over the chicken then squeeze until the chicken is completely seasoned.
5. Prick the chicken with skewers then set aside.
6. Preheat an Air Fryer to 375°F (191°C).
7. Arrange the chicken satay in the Air Fryer then pour the liquid over the chicken satay. Cook for 18 minutes.
8. Once it is done, remove the chicken satay from the Air Fryer then arrange on a serving dish.
9. Drizzle the gravy over the chicken satay then serve. Enjoy!

Nutritional Information:

Calories: 400, Fat: 31.7g, Protein: 22.4g, Carbs: 6.9g

Chicken Cilantro with Green Butter

Servings: 8

Ingredients:

- 8 chicken drumsticks
- 1 c. fresh cilantro
- 1 jalapeno
- 2 tbsps. minced garlic
- 2 tsps. ginger
- 2½ tbsps. extra virgin olive oil
- 1½ c. butter
- 1¾ tsps. salt
- ½ tsp. coriander
- ½ tsp. pepper
- ¼ c. lemon juice

Directions:

1. Chop ½ c. fresh cilantro and jalapeno then place in a bowl.
2. Add minced garlic, ginger, 1 ½ tsp. salt, olive oil, and 2 tbsp.s lemon juice to the bowl. Mix well.
3. Rub the chicken drumsticks with the cilantro mixture then marinate for at least an hour to overnight. Refrigerate to stay fresh.
4. After an hour, remove the seasoned drumsticks from the fridge then thaw at room temperature.
5. Preheat an Air Fryer to 400°F (204°C).
6. Place the chicken drumsticks in the Air Fryer then cook for 18 minutes.
7. Meanwhile, place butter and the remaining fresh cilantro in a bowl.
8. Season with the remaining salt, coriander, and pepper then pour lemon juice into the bowl.
9. Using an immersion blender blend the mixture until smooth and incorporated and smooth. Set aside.
10. Once the chicken drumsticks are done, remove from the Air Fryer then place on a serving dish.
11. Serve with the green cilantro butter then enjoy immediately.

Nutritional Information:

Calories: 399, Fat: 37.1g, Protein: 16.3g, Carbs: 1.4g

Refreshing Chicken Steak Tomato

Servings: 8

Ingredients:

- 1 lb. boneless chicken breast
- ½ tsp. salt
- ½ tsp. pepper
- 1 c. butter
- 1 c. diced tomatoes
- ½ tsp. nutmeg
- 1 bay leaf
- 1½ tsps. paprika
- ½ tsp. cloves
- ½ tsp. cayenne

Directions:

1. Preheat an Air Fryer to 375°F (191°C).
2. Cut the chicken breast into thick slices then arrange in the Air Fryer.
3. Sprinkle salt and pepper over the chicken then cook for 15 minutes.
4. Meanwhile, melt butter over low heat then add diced tomatoes to the melted butter.
5. Season with nutmeg, bay leaf, paprika, cloves, and cayenne then bring to a simmer.
6. Once it is done, remove the sauce from heat then let it cool.
7. When the chicken is done, remove from the Air Fryer then place on a serving dish.
8. Top with tomato sauce then serves right away.

Nutritional Information:

Calories: 361, Fat: 33g, Protein: 18.1g, Carbs: 2g

Crispy Fried Chicken

Servings: 8

Ingredients:

- 1 lb. chicken thighs
- 1 tsp. salt
- 1 tsp. pepper
- 1 c. almond flour
- 1 c. water
- 2 c. roasted pecans
- 1 tsp. black pepper

Directions:

1. Apply pepper and salt to the chicken thighs for seasoning and let sit for 5 minutes.
2. Meanwhile, place roasted pecans in a food processor then process until smooth and becoming flour.
3. Roll the seasoned chicken thighs in the almond flour then dip in the water.
4. Combine the remaining almond flour with pecans flour then mix well.
5. Remove the chicken thighs from water then roll in the pecans mixture. Using your finger squeeze the chicken thighs until all sides of the chicken thighs are completely coated with pecans mixture.
6. Preheat an Air Fryer to 400°F (204°C).
7. Arrange the coated chicken thighs in the Air Fryer then set the time to 22 minutes.
8. Once it is done, check the doneness of the chicken thighs. Give the chicken thighs an additional 5 minutes in the Air Fryer for a more golden brown color.
9. Place the crispy fried chicken on a serving dish then sprinkle black pepper on top.
10. Serve and enjoy hot.

Nutritional Information:

Calories: 455, Fat: 41.7g, Protein: 18g, Carbs: 6.3g

Oregano Chicken Rolls

Servings: 8

Ingredients:

- ½ lb. boneless chicken breast
- 1 tsp. oregano
- 2½ tsps. paprika
- 1½ tsps. minced garlic
- ¾ tsp. cumin
- ½ tsp. salt
- ½ tsp. pepper
- 1 tsp. extra virgin olive oil
- 1 bell pepper
- 1 onion
- 1 c. grated cheddar cheese
- ¼ c. butter
- ¼ c. Greek yogurt
- 1 egg yolk
- 2 c. roasted
- pecans

Directions:

1. Cut the chicken breast into large-thin slices.
2. Rub the chicken with oregano, paprika, minced garlic, cumin, salt, and pepper. Set aside.
3. Cut the bell pepper into sticks then set aside.
4. Peel and chop the onion then also set aside.
5. Place a chicken slice on a flat surface then arrange bell pepper stick, chopped onion, and grated cheddar cheese on it.
6. Roll the chicken then prick with a toothpick. Repeat with the remaining chicken and filling.
7. Place butter in a microwave-safe bowl then melts the butter.
8. Take the melted butter out of the microwave then add egg yolk and Greek yogurt to the melted butter. Stir until incorporated then set aside.
9. Next, place roasted pecans in a food processor then process until smooth and becoming flour form.
10. Take a chicken roll then dip in the butter mixture.
11. Roll the chicken in the pecans flour then set aside. Repeat with remaining chicken rolls.
12. Preheat an Air Fryer to 375°F (191°C).
13. Arrange the chicken roll in the Air Fryer then spray with olive oil.
14. Cook the chicken roll for 14 minutes then transfer to a serving dish.
15. Serve and enjoy.

Nutritional Information:

Calories: 393, Fat: 35g, Protein: 15.9g, Carbs: 7.5g

Buttery Whole Chicken

Servings: 4

Ingredients:

- 1 whole chicken
- ½ c. butter
- 1 tsp. black pepper
- 3 tbsps. minced garlic

Directions:

1. Place butter in mixing bowl then add minced garlic and black pepper.
2. Using a hand mixer beat the butter until combined.
3. Smear the chicken with the butter mixture and drop the remaining butter in the chicken cavity.
4. Preheat an Air Fryer to 350°F (177°C).
5. Place the chicken in the Air Fryer then cook for 30 minutes.
6. After 30 minutes, flip the chicken and cook again for another 30 minutes.
7. Once the internal temperature of the chicken has reached 165°F (74°C), remove it from the Air Fryer.
8. Allow the chicken to settle for a few minutes then serve.
9. Enjoy warm.

Nutritional Information:

Calories: 274, Fat: 27.6g, Protein: 5.5g, Carbs: 2.4g

Turkey Cilantro Creamy Butter

Servings: 4

Ingredients:

- 1 lb. turkey breast
- ½ c. cilantro
- 1 tsp. minced garlic
- ¾ tsp. cumin
- ¼ tsp. salt
- ½ tsp. pepper
- 2 tbsps. extra virgin olive oil
- ¼ c. chicken broth
- 2 tbsps. lemon juice
- ½ c. butter
- ½ tsp. garlic powder
- ¼ c. grated Parmesan cheese

Directions:

1. Cut the turkey breast into slices then set aside.
2. Combine cilantro with minced garlic, cumin, salt, and pepper then pour olive oil, chicken broth, and lemon juice into the mixing bowl. Stir until incorporated.
3. Rub the turkey breast with the spice mixture then let it sit for about 30 minutes. Store in the fridge to keep it fresh.
4. Meanwhile, combine butter with garlic powder and Parmesan cheese then using an electric mixer mix until combined and fluffy. Set aside.
5. After 30 minutes of seasoning process, take the turkey out of the fridge.
6. Preheat an Air Fryer to 350°F (177°C) and place a rack in the Air Fryer.
7. Place the seasoned turkey on the rack then cook for 20 minutes.
8. Open the Air Fryer then flip the turkey. Cook the turkey again for another 20 minutes.
9. Once it is done, remove the turkey from the Air Fryer then place on a serving dish.
10. Serve and enjoy with creamy butter.

Nutritional Information:

Calories: 402, Fat: 36.3g, Protein: 16.8g, Carbs: 4.1g

Turkey Breast with Strawberry Glaze

Servings: 4

Ingredients:

- 2 lbs. turkey breast
- 1 tsp. salt
- ¾ tsp. black pepper
- 1 tbsp. olive oil
- 1 c. fresh strawberries
- 2 tbsps. chopped shallots
- 2 tbsps. lemon juice
- 1 tbsp. coconut flour
- ¼ c. chicken broth
- ½ c. butter

Directions:

1. Season the turkey breast with salt and black pepper.
2. Preheat an Air Fryer to 375°F (191°C).
3. Place the turkey in the Air Fryer then cook for 15 minutes.
4. While waiting for the turkey, pour chicken broth into a saucepan then add shallots and lemon juice. Bring to boil.
5. Once it is boiled, stir in coconut flour then stir until incorporated and smooth.
6. Add butter to the saucepan then cook until the butter is melted. Remove from heat then set aside.
7. After 15 minutes of cooking time, open the Air Fryer then flip the turkey. Cook the turkey for another 15 minutes.
8. Meanwhile, place the fresh strawberries in a food processor. Process until smooth.
9. Drizzle the strawberry over the turkey then cook again for 7 minutes.
10. Remove the turkey from heat then serve with the sauce.
11. Enjoy!

Nutritional Information:

Calories: 344, Fat: 28.3g, Protein: 15.7g, Carbs: 7.8g

Seafood

Nutty Shrimps with Chili Sauce

Servings: 4

Ingredients:

- 1 lb. fresh shrimps
- 1 egg white
- ½ c. almond flour
- 1 c. roasted pecans
- 1 tsp. paprika
- ¼ tsp. salt
- 1 tsp. pepper
- ½ c. Greek yogurt
- 2 tbsps. chili sauce

Directions:

1. Peel the fresh shrimps then discard the head. Set aside.
2. Season the egg white with salt and paprika then whisk to combine.
3. Place roasted pecans in a food processor then season with pepper. Process until smooth and becoming flour.
4. Roll the shrimps in the almond flour then dip in the seasoned egg white.
5. Next, roll the shrimps again in the pecans mixture then set aside. Repeat with the remaining shrimps and flour.
6. Preheat an Air Fryer to 400°F (204°C).
7. Arrange the coated shrimps in the Air Fryer then spray with cooking spray.
8. Cook the shrimps for 5 minutes then arrange on a serving dish.
9. Combine Greek yogurt with chili sauce then mix until incorporated.
10. Drizzle the chili yogurt mixture over the shrimps then serves. Enjoy right away.

Nutritional Information:

Calories: 288, Fat: 23.9g, Protein: 16g, Carbs: 6.4g

Soft Lemon Crab Cakes

Servings: 8

Ingredients:

- 1 lb. crabmeat
- 2½ tbsps. lemon juice
- ½ c. diced bell pepper
- ¼ c. chopped onion
- 1 c. mayonnaise
- 1 tbsp. yellow mustard
- 1½ tsps. black pepper
- 1½ tbsps. chopped parsley
- 1¼ tsps. garlic powder
- ¼ tsp. cayenne pepper
- 2 tbsps. extra virgin olive oil
- ½ c. roasted walnuts

Directions:

1. Put your walnuts which are roasted in a blender then process until smooth.
2. Add crabmeat to the food processor then season with lemon juice, yellow mustard, black pepper, garlic powder, and cayenne pepper. Process until smooth.
3. Transfer the crab and walnuts mixture to a bowl then add chopped onion and diced bell pepper to the mixture.
4. Pour mayonnaise over the mixture then mix well.
5. Split the mixture into 16 then roll into balls.
6. Press each ball using your hands until becoming patty form. Repeat with the remaining patties.
7. Preheat an Air Fryer to 375°F (191°C).
8. Arrange the patties in the Air Fryer then spray with extra virgin olive oil.
9. Cook the patties for 10 minutes. You may cook them in two batches.
10. Once it is done, remove the cooked crab patties from the Air Fryer then serve.
11. Enjoy immediately.

Nutritional Information:

Calories: 246, Fat: 20.3g, Protein: 10.1g, Carbs: 4.2g

Fried Shrimps with Avocado Topping

Servings: 8

Ingredients:

- 2 lbs. fresh shrimps
- 2 tsps. extra virgin olive oil
- ½ c. chopped onion
- 2 tbsps. chopped celeries
- 2 tbsps. diced paprika
- ¼ tsp. salt
- ½ tsp. pepper
- 1 ripe avocado
- ½ c. chopped roasted pecans

Directions:

1. Preheat an Air Fryer to 400°F (204°C).
2. Place chopped onion in the Air Fryer then spray with extra virgin olive oil. Cook the onion for 5 minutes.
3. Next, add fresh shrimps to the Air Fryer then cook for another 5 minutes.
4. After that, add chopped celeries and paprika to the Air Fryer then season with salt and pepper. Mix well.
5. Let the Air Fryer at 400°F (204°) and cook the ingredients for 5 minutes.
6. Once it is done, transfer the cooked shrimps and the other ingredients to a serving dish.
7. Peel the ripe avocado then discard the seed. Cut into cubes.
8. Sprinkle avocado cubes, and chopped roasted pecans on top then serve.
9. Enjoy!

Nutritional Information:

Calories: 248, Fat: 20.9g, Protein: 7.8g, Carbs: 9.9g

Cod Coconut Fritter

Servings: 8

Ingredients:

- 1 lb. cod fillet
- ¼ c. grated coconut
- ½ c. grated cheddar cheese
- 2 tbsps. lemon juice
- ¼ tsp. grated lemon zest
- 1 tbsp. chopped parsley
- 2 tsps. minced garlic
- 2 tsps. paprika
- ¼ c. butter
- ½ c. mayonnaise

Directions:

1. Allow the butter to melt in the microwave then let it cool.
2. Cut the cod fillet into cubes then place in a food processor.
3. Add grated coconut to the food processor then season with lemon juice, grated lemon zest, chopped parsley, minced garlic, and paprika. Process until smooth.
4. Add melted butter to the mixture then mix well.
5. Shape the cod mixture into fritters form then let them sit.
6. Preheat an Air Fryer to 380°F (191).
7. Arrange the cod fritter in the Air Fryer then cook for 6 minutes.
8. After 6 minutes, flip the fritter then cook again for another 6 minutes.
9. Once it is done, remove from the Air Fryer then serve with mayonnaise.
10. Enjoy!

Nutritional Information:

Calories: 348, Fat: 27.4g, Protein: 19.3g, Carbs: 9.7g

Crispy Shrimps Coconuts

Servings: 6

Ingredients:

- 1 lb. fresh shrimps
- 1 tsp. salt
- 1 tsp. pepper
- 1 c. coconut flour
- 2 eggs
- 2 c. grated coconuts
- 2 tbsps. butter
- 2 tsps. minced garlic
- ½ c. cilantro
- 1 c. coconut milk
- 2 tbsps. lemon juice

Directions:

1. Peel the fresh shrimps then discard the head.
2. Rub the peeled shrimps with salt and pepper then let it sit for 5 minutes.
3. Prepare coconut flour, beaten eggs, and grated coconuts in three different bowls in a row.
4. Roll the fresh shrimps in the coconut flour then dip in beaten eggs.
5. Take the shrimps out of the beaten eggs then roll in the grated coconuts. Using your finger squeeze the shrimps until all sides of the shrimps are completely coated with grated coconuts.
6. Preheat an Air Fryer to 400°F (204°C).
7. Arrange the shrimps in the Air Fryer then set the time to 10 minutes.
8. Once it is done, check the color of the shrimps. Cook the shrimps for 2 minutes more for a more golden brown color.
9. Place the crispy fried shrimps in a serving dish then serve.
10. Enjoy right away or serve with tomato sauce.

Nutritional Information:

Calories: 342, Fat: 27.1g, Protein: 19.5g, Carbs: 6g

Calamari Crispy with Lemon Butter

Servings: 8

Ingredients:

- 1 lb. fresh squids
- 1 tsp. salt
- 1 tsp. pepper
- 2 c. almond flour
- 1 c. water
- 1 c. butter
- 1½ tbsps. mustard
- 2 tsps. lemon juice

Directions:

1. Peel the outer skin of the squids then discard the ink.
2. Cut the squids into rings then rub with salt and pepper.
3. Roll the seasoned squids in the almond flour then dip in the water.
4. Return the squids to the almond flour then roll until the squids are completely coated with almond flour.
5. Preheat an Air Fryer to 400°F (204°C).
6. Place the coated squids in the Air Fryer then cook for 6 minutes.
7. Once it is done, remove from the Air Fryer then place on a serving dish.
8. Place butter in a mixing bowl then adds mustard and juice from the lemon.
9. Mix until smooth and fluffy.
10. Serve the fried calamari with the lemon butter.
11. Enjoy!

Nutritional Information:

Calories: 429, Fat: 38.7g, Protein: 16.3g, Carbs: 8.2g

Servings: 4

Ingredients:

- ½ lb. tuna steak
- 1 tbsp. lemon juice
- 1 egg
- 1 c. roasted pecans
- 1 tsp. ginger
- ½ tsp. chili powder
- ¼ tsp. salt
- ¼ tsp. pepper
- 1 tsp. extra virgin olive oil

Directions:

1. Splash lemon juice over the tuna then let it rest for a few minutes.
2. Next, crack the egg then place in a bowl.
3. Season the egg with salt, pepper, and chili powder then stir until incorporated. Set aside.
4. Place roasted pecans in a food processor then process until becoming flour texture.
5. After that, add ginger to the pecans then process again until combined. Transfer the pecans mixture to a bowl.
6. Mix the tuna in the egg mixture then roll in the pecan mixture.
7. Return to the egg mixture then roll again in the pecan mixture. Make sure that all sides of the tuna are completely coated with pecan.
8. Preheat an Air Fryer to 400°F (204°C) and place a rack in it.
9. Once the Air Fryer is ready, place the coated tuna on the rack then cook for 5 minutes.
10. Flip the tuna and cook again for another 5 minutes. The tuna will be lightly golden brown.
11. Remove the fried tuna from the Air Fryer then place in a serving dish.
12. Serve and enjoy.

Nutritional Information:

Calories: 313, Fat: 28g, Protein: 14.4g, Carbs: 4.6g

Fried Shrimps Garlic

Servings: 2

Ingredients:

- 1 lb. fresh shrimps
- ¼ tsp. salt
- 1 tbsp. coriander
- 3 tbsps. minced garlic
- 1 tsp. extra virgin olive oil
- ¼ c. butter
- 1½ tsps. cayenne
- 1 tsp. smoked paprika
- 1½ tbsps. Worcestershire sauce
- 2 tsps. lemon juice
- 1 tsp. ginger

Directions:

1. Peel the shrimps then remove the head.
2. Season the shrimp with coriander, minced garlic, and salt. Let the shrimps rest for at least 10 minutes.
3. Place butter in a mixing bowl then adds cayenne, smoked paprika, Worcestershire sauce, ginger, and lemon juice.
4. Use an electric mixer to beat butter until it attains a creamy and smooth consistency. Set aside.
5. Preheat an Air Fryer to 400°F (204°C) and put a rack in it.
6. Place the seasoned shrimps on the rack then cook for 5 minutes.
7. Remove the cooked shrimps from the Air Fryer then serve with creamy hot butter.

Nutritional Information:

Calories: 396, Fat: 31.5g, Protein: 19.4g, Carbs: 6.8g

Buttered Scallops with Thyme

Servings: 2

Ingredients:

- 1 lb. scallops
- ½ tbsp. butter
- ½ c. chopped fresh thyme
- ¼ tsp. salt
- ½ tsp. pepper

Directions:

1. Remove the shells of the scallops then wash and rinse them.
2. Season the scallops with salt and pepper then set aside.
3. Drop butter on several places in a disposable aluminum pan then sprinkles thyme on it.
4. Arrange the scallops on the thyme then set aside.
5. Preheat an Air Fryer to 400°F (204°C) and place a rack in the Air Fryer.
6. Set the time to 7 minutes then cook the scallops.
7. Once the scallops are done, remove from the Air Fryer then transfer to a serving dish together with the liquid and thyme.
8. Serve and enjoy.

Nutritional Information:

Calories: 264, Fat: 24,2g, Protein: 6.4g, Carbs: 8.7g

Hot Mackerel Chili

Servings: 2

Ingredients:

- 2 medium mackerels
- 1 tbsp. extra virgin olive oil
- 1 tsp. lemon juice
- 2 tsps. minced garlic
- 2 tbsps. red chili flakes
- ¼ tsp. salt
- 1 tbsp. butter

Directions:

1. Splash lemon juice over the mackerels then let it rest for about 5 minutes.
2. Rub the mackerels with minced garlic, red chili flakes, and salt then set aside.
3. Preheat an Air Fryer to 350°F (177°C).
4. Once the Air Fryer is ready, place the seasoned mackerels in the Air Fryer then cook for 5 minutes.
5. After 5 minutes, open the drawer and flip the mackerels. Cook again for another 5 minutes.
6. Remove the cooked mackerels from the Air Fryer then place on a rack.
7. Quickly brush the cooked mackerels with butter then serve.
8. Enjoy!

Nutritional Information:

Calories: 413, Fat: 37.1g, Protein: 21g, Carbs: 0.7g

Halibut Cheesy Lemon

Servings: 6

Ingredients:

- 1 lb. halibut fillet
- ¼ tsp. salt
- ¼ tsp. pepper
- 1 tbsp. extra virgin olive oil
- ¾ c. grated Parmesan cheese
- ½ c. butter
- 2½ tbsps. mayonnaise
- 2½ tbsps. lemon juice
- ¼ c. chopped onion

Directions:

1. Brush the halibut fillet with olive oil then season with salt and pepper.
2. Preheat an Air Fryer to 375°F (191°C).
3. Once the Air Fryer is ready, place the seasoned halibut fillet in the Air Fryer and cook for 12 minutes.
4. Meanwhile, place butter in a mixing bowl then pours lemon juice over the butter.
5. Add mayonnaise to the mixing bowl then using an electric mixer beat the butter until smooth and creamy.
6. Next, stir in grated Parmesan cheese, and chopped onion then mixes well.
7. After 12 minutes of cooking time, open the drawer then spread the butter mixture over the cooked halibut.
8. Allow cooking for two minutes then remove from the Air Fryer.
9. Transfer the cooked halibut to a serving dish then serve.
10. Enjoy right away.

Nutritional Information:

Calories: 346, Fat: 31.2g, Protein: 15g, Carbs: 1.1g

Scallops with Lemon Parsley Butter

Servings: 4

Ingredients:

- 1 lb. scallops
- 1 tbsp. lemon juice
- ¼ tsp. salt
- ¼ sp. pepper
- 1½ tbsps. extra virgin olive oil
- ¼ c. chopped parsley
- ½ c. butter
- ½ tsp. grated lemon zest

Directions:

1. Wash scallops then pat them dry.
2. Splash lemon juice over the scallops then seasons with salt and pepper.
3. Marinate the scallops for an hour and store in the refrigerator to keep them fresh.
4. After an hour, remove the scallops from the refrigerator then thaw at room temperature. Transfer the scallops to an aluminum pan.
5. Preheat an Air Fryer to 400°F (204°C) and place a rack in it.
6. Place the aluminum pan with scallops on the rack then cook for 5 minutes.
7. Remove the scallops from the Air Fryer then transfer to a serving dish.
8. Melt butter in a saucepan then removes from heat.
9. Add chopped parsley, and grated lemon zest then stir until thickened.
10. Drizzle the butter over the scallops then serve.
11. Enjoy right away.

Nutritional Information:

Calories: 307, Fat: 28.8g, Protein: 11.1g, Carbs: 2g

Pork and Lamb

Spicy Glazed Pork Loaf

Servings: 8

Ingredients:

- 1½ c. ground pork
- ½ c. diced pork rinds
- ½ tsp. paprika
- ½ tsp. pepper
- 2 tsps. minced garlic
- ½ c. chopped onion
- ½ tsp. cumin
- ½ tsp. cayenne
- ¼ c. butter
- ½ c. tomato puree
- ½ tsp. chili powder
- 2 tbsps. coconut aminos
- ½ tsp. Worcestershire sauce
- 1 tsp. lemon juice

Directions:

1. Combine ground pork and pork rinds in a bowl then season with paprika, pepper, minced garlic, cumin, cayenne, and chopped onion. Mix well.
2. Transfer the pork mixture to a silicone loaf pan then spread evenly. Set aside.
3. Next, melt the butter in microwave then set aside.
4. Combine the melted butter with tomato puree, chili powder, coconut aminos, Worcestershire sauce, and lemon juice. Stir until incorporated.
5. Drizzle the glaze mixture over the pork loaf then set aside.
6. Preheat an Air Fryer to 350°F (177°C).
7. Once the Air Fryer is preheated, place the silicon loaf pan on the Air Fryer's rack then cook for 20 minutes.
8. Remove from the Air Fryer then let it cool.
9. Cut the pork loaf into slices then serve.

Nutritional Information:

Calories: 255, Fat: 20.1g, Protein: 13g, Carbs: 6g

Baby Back Ribs Tender

Servings: 2

Ingredients:

- 2 baby back ribs
- ½ tsp. salt
- 3 tsps. grated garlic
- ¾ tsp. ginger
- ¾ tsp. pepper
- 2 tsps. red chili flakes
- 1 tbsp. extra virgin olive oil

Directions:

1. Combine salt, grated garlic, ginger, pepper, and red chili flakes in a bowl then mix well.
2. Rub the baby back ribs with the spice mixture then set aside.
3. Preheat an Air Fryer to 350°F (177°C).
4. Place the seasoned baby back ribs and set the time to 30 minutes. Cook the baby back ribs.
5. Once it is done, remove from the Air Fryer then transfer to a serving dish.
6. Serve and enjoy immediately.

Nutritional Information:

Calories: 409, Fat: 34.3g, Protein: 19.3g, Carbs: 6.3g

Pork Roast with Thai Walnuts Sauce

Servings: 2

Ingredients:

- 1 pork roast
- ½ tsp. salt
- 1 tbsp. extra virgin olive oil
- ½ tsp. pepper
- 1 tsp. thyme
- 1 tsp. rosemary
- 6 cloves garlic
- ½ c. butter

- 3 tbsps. roasted walnuts
- 3 tbsps. low sodium chicken broth
- 2 tbsps. lemon juice
- ½ tsp. ginger
- 2 tbsps. minced garlic

Directions:

1. Place butter in a mixing bowl then adds roasted walnuts, ginger, and minced garlic.
2. Pour chicken broth and lemon juice into the mixing bowl then using an electric mixer beat until smooth.
3. Transfer the butter mixture to a container with a lid then store in a refrigerator overnight.
4. Preheat an Air Fryer to 350°F (177°C) and put garlic in the Air Fryer.
5. Brush the pork roast with olive oil then place in the Air Fryer after the garlic.
6. Sprinkle salt, pepper, thyme, and rosemary then cook for 30 minutes.
7. Once it is done, remove from the Air Fryer then place on a serving dish.
8. Serve with walnut sauce.

Nutritional Information:

Calories: 325, Fat: 32.6g, Protein: 6.7g, Carbs: 3.2g

Pork Butt Onion Barbecue

Servings: 2

Ingredients:

- ½ lb. pork butt
- 1 tbsp. extra virgin olive oil
- ½ tsp. salt
- ½ tsp. pepper
- ½ c. chopped onion
- 2 tbsps. tomato sauce
- ½ tsp. cider vinegar
- ½ tsp. chili powder
- 1 tsp. cayenne pepper
- ½ tsp. garlic powder
- ½ tsp. onion powder
- 2½ tbsps. Worcestershire sauce
- ½ tsp. mustard
- 1 tbsp. Stevia

Direction:

1. Combine tomato sauce with cider vinegar, chili powder, cayenne pepper, garlic powder, onion powder, Worcestershire sauce, mustard, and Stevia in a bowl then stir until incorporated. Set aside.
2. Preheat an Air Fryer to 350°F (177°C).
3. Spray the pork but with olive oil then season with salt and pepper.
4. Place the seasoned pork in the Air Fryer then sprinkle chopped onion on top.
5. Cook the pork butt and set the time to 6 minutes.
6. After 6 minutes, open the drawer and flip the pork.
7. Drizzle the sauce over the pork butt then cook again for 6 minutes.
8. Once it is done, remove from the Air Fryer and transfer to a serving dish.
9. Serve and enjoy.

Nutritional Information:

Calories: 459, Fat: 38.1g, Protein: 20.6g, Carbs: 9.2g

Pork Shoulder with Zucchini Salads

Servings: 2

Ingredients:

- ½ pork shoulder
- 3 tbsps. extra virgin olive oil
- 2 tsp. salt
- 1 c. sliced zucchini
- ¼ c. chopped onion
- ½ c. diced bell pepper
- 1 tbsp. chopped basil
- 1 tbsp. sesame oil
- 1 tbsp. lemon juice

Directions:

1. Score the pork shoulder on several places then rub it with salt and olive oil. Repeat for three times.
2. Preheat an Air Fryer to 300°F (148°C).
3. Place the seasoned pork shoulder in the Air Fryer then cook for thirty mins.
4. Once 30 minutes are over, increase the temperature to 400°F (204°C) and cook again for 20 minutes.
5. Meanwhile, place sliced zucchinis, chopped onion, diced bell pepper, and chopped basil in a salad bowl.
6. Sprinkle sesame oil and lemon juice over the salads then toss to combine. Store in the refrigerator.
7. Once the pork shoulder is done, remove from the Air Fryer and let it sit for about 10 minutes.
8. Cut into slices then arrange on a serving dish.
9. Serve with zucchini salads.

Nutritional Information:

Calories: 372, Fat: 35.1g, Protein: 11.2g, Carbs: 5.7g

Lamb Curry in Wrap

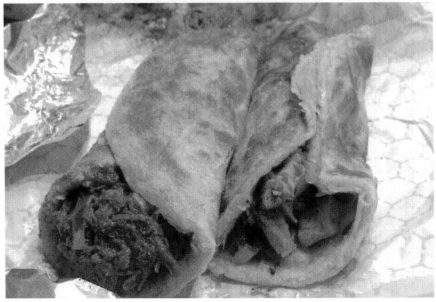

Servings: 8

Ingredients:

- 1 lb. lamb loin
- 1 tbsp. extra virgin olive oil
- 1 c. chopped onion
- 2 tbsps. sliced shallots
- 1 c. chopped leek
- 1 tsp. curry powder
- ½ tsp. turmeric
- 1 tsp. black pepper
- ½ tsp. salt
- ¼ c. coconut milk
- 1 c. coconut flour
- 3 egg yolks
- 2 c. water

Directions:

1. Place the lamb loin a food processor then process until smooth.
2. Place the ground lamb in a bowl then add chopped onion, sliced shallots, and chopped leek to the bowl.
3. Season with curry powder, turmeric, salt, and pepper then pour a ½ tbsp. of olive oil and coconut milk to the bowl. Mix well.
4. Preheat an Air Fryer to 400°F (204°C).
5. Transfer the lamb mixture to the Air Fryer then cook for 15 minutes.
6. Meanwhile, combine coconut flour with egg yolks and water then stir until smooth and incorporated.
7. Using a saucepan make 8 thin omelets then set aside.
8. When the lamb is cooked through, transfer to a bowl.
9. Take a sheet of coconut flour omelet then place on a flat surface.
10. Drop 2 tbsps. of cooked lamb on the omelets then fold until becoming a tight roll. Repeat with the remaining lamb and coconut flour omelet.
11. Preheat the Air Fryer again to 375°F (191°C).
12. Arrange the lamb rolls in the Air Fryer then spray with the remaining olive oil.

13. Cook the lamb rolls for 10 minutes then remove from the Air Fryer. If you like the lamb rolls to be more golden brown, cook the lamb rolls for another 5 minutes.
14. Serve and enjoy.

Nutritional Information:

Calories: 276, Fat: 21,8g, Protein: 13.8g, Carbs: 5.4g

Lamb Sirloin Steak with Parsley Sauce

Servings: 8

Ingredients:

- 1 lb. lamb sirloin
- ½ c. chopped onion
- 3 tsps. ginger
- 4 tsps. minced garlic
- 1½ tsps. fennel
- 1½ tsps. cinnamon
- ¾ tsp. cardamom
- 2½ tsps. cayenne
- ¾ tsp. salt
- 1 c. butter

- ¼ c. chopped scallions
- 3 tsps. minced garlic
- ¼ c. chopped parsley
- ¾ tsp. chives
- 1½ tsps. horseradish
- 1¼ tsps. thyme
- ¾ tsp. paprika
- ¼ tsp. pepper

Directions:

1. Place chopped onion, ginger, garlic, fennel, cinnamon, cardamom, cayenne, and salt in a food processor. Process until smooth.
2. Cut the lamb sirloin into thin slices then rub with the spice mixture. Marinate the lamb sirloin for at least 30 minutes.
3. After 30 minutes, preheat an Air Fryer to 400°F (204°C).
4. Place the seasoned sliced lamb in the Air Fryer then cook for 15 minutes.
5. Meanwhile, melt butter in a saucepan then stir in minced garlic to the saucepan. Sauté until aromatic.
6. Add scallions, parsley, chives, horseradish, thyme, paprika, and pepper then stir until thickened.
7. Get the sauce off heat then let it cool.
8. When the lamb is cooked, transfer to a serving dish.
9. Drizzle parsley sauce on top then serve.
10. Enjoy with roasted vegetables or any kinds of side dish, as you desired.

Nutritional Information:

Calories: 358, Fat: 37.1g, Protein: 5.1g, Carbs: 3g

Lamb Chop Garlic and Avocado Mayo

Servings: 2

Ingredients:

- 2 lamb chops
- 2 tsps. minced garlic
- ¾ tbsp. oregano
- ¼ tsp. salt
- ½ tsp. black pepper
- 2 ripe avocados
- ½ c. mayonnaise
- 2 tbsps. cilantro
- 1 tbsp. lemon juice

Directions:

1. Season the lamb chops with minced garlic, oregano, salt, and black pepper. Let them rest for about 5 minutes.
2. Preheat an Air Fryer to 400°F (204°C) and place a rack in it.
3. Once the Air Fryer is ready, place the seasoned lamb chops on the rack then cook for 12 minutes.
4. Meanwhile, cut the avocados into halves then discard the seeds.
5. Scoop out the avocado flesh then place in a blender.
6. Add cilantro, mayonnaise, and lemon juice to the blender then blend until smooth and creamy.
7. Once the lamb chops are done, remove from the Air Fryer and transfer to a serving dish.
8. Serve and enjoy with the Avocado Mayonnaise.

Nutritional Information:

Calories: 398, Fat: 35.6g, Protein: 11.5g, Carbs: 10g

Spicy Lamb Curry Rolls

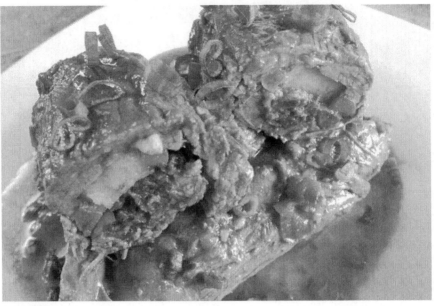

Servings: 2

Ingredients:

- ½ lb. boneless lamb loin
- 2 tbsps. butter
- ½ c. chopped onion
- 2 tsps. minced garlic
- ¼ tsp. salt
- ¼ tsp. pepper
- ½ tsp. turmeric
- 1 tsp. curry powder
- 1 tsp. red chili flakes
- ½ tsp. cayenne
- ½ c. coconut milk
- ½ lb. steamed cabbage
- 2 tbsps. extra virgin olive oil

Directions:

1. Cut the lamb loin into small dices then set aside.
2. Preheat a skillet over medium heat then melt butter in it.
3. Stir in minced garlic, and chopped onion then sauté until aromatic.
4. Add diced lamb then season with salt, pepper, turmeric, curry powder, and red chili flakes then pour coconut milk over the lamb.
5. Allow cooking till the liquid is absorbed into the lamb then remove from heat.
6. Lay a sheet of steamed cabbage then put 2 tbsps of lamb curry on it.
7. Wrap the lamb with cabbage and roll it tightly. Repeat with the remaining cabbage and lamb.
8. Preheat an Air Fryer to 375°F (191°C) and place a rack in it.
9. Wait until the Air Fryer reaches the desired temperature then arrange the cabbage roll on the rack.
10. Cook the cabbage rolls and set the time to 15 minutes.
11. Once the cabbage rolls are done, remove from the Air Fryer then arrange on a serving dish.
12. Serve and enjoy warm.

Nutritional Information:

Calories: 370, Fat: 33.2g, Protein: 11.6g, Carbs: 8.4g

Spiced Lamb Satay

Servings: 3

Ingredients:

- 2 boneless lamb shoulders
- ½ tsp. salt
- ½ tsp. pepper
- 1 tsp. ginger
- ½ tsp. nutmeg
- ¼ tsp. cumin
- 2 kaffir lime leaves
- 2 lemongrasses
- 1-tbsp. extra virgin olive oil

Directions:

1. Place salt, pepper, ginger, nutmeg, and cumin in a bowl then mix well.
2. Cut the lamb shoulder into medium cubes then rub with the spice mixture.
3. Marinate the lamb cubes for 10 minutes then prick using steel skewers.
4. Preheat an Air Fryer to 400°F (204°C) and arrange the lamb satay in the Air Fryer.
5. Spray the lamb satay with olive oil then put lime leaves and lemon grasses on top.
6. Cook the lamb satay and set the time to 8 minutes.
7. Once it is done, remove from the Air Fryer and enjoy with any kind of low carb sauce, as you desired.

Nutritional Information:

Calories: 249, Fat: 20.2g, Protein: 12.9g, Carbs: 3.7g

Easy Lamb Ribs with Minty Yogurt

Servings: 1

Ingredients:

- 1 lb. lamb ribs
- ½ tsp. salt
- ½ tsp. pepper
- 2 tbsps. mustard
- 1 tsp. chopped rosemary
- 1 c. Greek yogurt
- ¼ c. chopped mint leaves

Directions:

1. Brush mustard over the lamb ribs then sprinkles salt, pepper, and rosemary over the lamb.
2. Preheat an Air Fryer to 350°F (177°C).
3. Once the Air Fryer is ready, place the lamb ribs in the Air Fryer and set the time to 18 minutes.
4. In the meantime, combine yogurt with chopped mint leaves then stir well. Set aside.
5. Once the lamb ribs are done, remove from the Air Fryer and transfer to a serving dish.
6. Serve with minty yogurt then enjoy!
7. This lamb ribs will be great to be enjoyed with roasted vegetables.

Nutritional Information:

Calories: 163, Fat: 15.3g, Protein: 4.3g, Carbs: 4.4g

Veggies and Sides

Perfect Brussels sprout and Cheese

Servings: 2

Ingredients:

- ¾ c. Brussels sprouts
- 1 tbsp. extra virgin olive oil
- ¼ tsp. salt
- ¼ c. grated Mozzarella cheese

Directions:

1. Cut the Brussels sprouts into halves then place in a bowl.
2. Drizzle extra virgin olive oil over the Brussels sprouts then sprinkle salt on top. Toss to combine.
3. Preheat an Air Fryer to 375°F (191°C).
4. Transfer the seasoned Brussels sprouts to the Air Fryer then cook for 15 minutes.
5. After 15 minutes, open the Air Fryer and sprinkle grated Mozzarella cheese over the cooked Brussels sprouts.
6. Cook the Brussels sprouts in the Air Fryer for 5 minutes or until the Mozzarella cheese is melted.
7. Once it is done, remove from the Air Fryer then transfer to a serving dish.
8. Serve and enjoy with tomato sauce if you like.

Nutritional Information:

Calories: 224, Fat: 18.1g, Protein: 10.1g, Carbs: 4.5g

Cauliflower Florets in Curly Egg

Servings: 2

Ingredients:

- 2 c. cauliflower florets
- 3 tsps. minced garlic
- ½ tsp. salt
- ½ tsp. coriander
- 2 c. water
- 3 eggs
- ½ tsp. pepper
- ¼ c. grated Mozzarella cheese
- 2 tbsps. tomato puree

Directions:

1. Place minced garlic, salt, and coriander in a container then pour water into it. Stir until the seasoning is completely dissolved.
2. Add the cauliflower florets to the brine then submerge for at least 30 minutes.
3. After 30 minutes, remove the cauliflower florets from the brine then wash and rinse them. Pat them dry.
4. Preheat an Air Fryer to 400°F (204°C).
5. Crash the eggs and place in a bowl.
6. Season with pepper then whisks until incorporated.
7. Dip a cauliflower floret in the egg then place in the air fryer. Repeat with the remaining cauliflower florets and egg.
8. Cook the cauliflower florets for 12 minutes or until lightly golden and the egg is curly.
9. Sprinkle grated Mozzarella cheese then drizzle tomato puree on top.
10. Cook the cauliflower florets again for another 5 minutes then remove from the Air Fryer.
11. Transfer to a serving dish then serve. Enjoy warm.

Nutritional Information:

Calories: 276, Fat: 21.8g, Protein: 13.8g, Carbs: 5.4g

Fried Green Beans Rosemary

Servings: 2

Ingredients:

- ¾ c. chopped green beans
- 3 tsps. minced garlic
- 2 tbsps. rosemary
- ½ tsp. salt
- 1 tbsp. butter

Directions:

1. Preheat an Air Fryer to 390°F (200°C).
2. Place the chopped green beans in the Air Fryer then brush with butter.
3. Sprinkle salt, minced garlic, and rosemary over the green beans then cook for 5 minutes.
4. Once the green beans are done, remove from the Air Fryer then place on a serving dish.
5. Serve and enjoy warm.

Nutritional Information:

Calories: 72, Fat: 6.3g, Protein: 0.7g, Carbs: 4.5g

Crispy Broccoli Pop Corn

Servings: 4

Ingredients:

- 2 c. broccoli florets
- 2 c. coconut flour
- 4 egg yolks
- ½ tsp. salt
- ½ tsp. pepper
- ¼ c. butter

Directions:

1. Soak the broccoli florets in salty water to remove all the insects inside.
2. Wash and rinse the broccoli florets then pat them dry.
3. Melt butter then let it cool.
4. Crack the eggs then place in the same bowl with the melted butter.
5. Add coconut flour to the liquid then season with salt and pepper. Mix until incorporated.
6. Preheat an Air Fryer to 400°F (204°C).
7. Dip a broccoli floret in the coconut flour mixture then place in the Air Fryer. Repeat with the remaining broccoli florets.
8. Cook the broccoli florets 6 minutes. You may do this in several batches.
9. Once it is done, remove the fried broccoli popcorn from the Air Fryer then place on a serving dish.
10. Serve and enjoy immediately.

Nutritional Information:

Calories: 202, Fat: 17.5g, Protein: 5.1g, Carbs: 7.8g

Cheesy Cauliflower Croquettes

Servings: 4

Ingredients:

- 2 c. cauliflower florets
- 2 tsps. minced garlic
- ½ c. chopped onion
- ¾ tsp. mustard
- ½ tsp. salt
- ½ tsp. pepper
- 2 tbsps. butter
- ¾ c. grated cheddar cheese

Directions:

1. Place butter in a microwave-safe bowl then melts the butter. Let it cool.
2. Place cauliflower florets in a food processor then process until smooth and becoming crumbles.
3. Transfer the cauliflower crumbles to a bowl then add chopped onion and cheese.
4. Season with minced garlic, mustard, salt, and pepper then pour melted butter over the mixture.
5. Shape the cauliflower mixture into medium balls then arrange in the Air Fryer.
6. Preheat an Air Fryer to 400°F (204°C) and cook the cauliflower croquettes for 14 minutes.
7. To achieve a more golden brown color, cook the cauliflower croquettes for another 2 minutes.
8. Serve and enjoy with homemade tomato sauce.

Nutritional Information:

Calories: 160, Fat: 13g, Protein: 6.8g, Carbs: 5.1g

Spinach in Cheese Envelopes

Servings: 8

Ingredients:

- 3 c. cream cheese
- 1½ c. coconut flour
- 3 egg yolks
- 2 eggs
- ½ c. cheddar cheese
- 2 c. steamed spinach
- ¼ tsp. salt
- ½ tsp. pepper
- ¼ c. chopped onion

Directions:

1. Place cream cheese in a mixing bowl then whisks until soft and fluffy.
2. Add egg yolks to the mixing bowl then continue whisking until incorporated.
3. Stir in coconut flour to the cheese mixture then mix until becoming a soft dough.
4. Place the dough on a flat surface then roll until thin.
5. Cut the thin dough into 8 squares then keep.
6. Crash the eggs then place in a bowl.
7. Season with salt, pepper, and grated cheese then mix well.
8. Add chopped spinach and onion to the egg mixture then stir until combined.
9. Put spinach filling on a square dough then fold until becoming an envelope. Repeat with the remaining spinach filling and dough. Glue with water.
10. Preheat an Air Fryer to 425°F (218°C).
11. Arrange the spinach envelopes in the Air Fryer then cook for 12 minutes or until lightly golden brown.
12. Remove from the Air Fryer then serve warm. Enjoy!

Nutritional Information:

Calories: 365, Fat: 34.6g, Protein: 10.4g, Carbs: 4.4g

Cheesy Mushroom Slices

Servings: 8

Ingredients:

- 2 c. chopped mushrooms
- 2 eggs
- ¾ c. almond flour
- ½ c. grated cheddar cheese
- 2 tbsps. butter
- ½ tsp. pepper
- ¼ tsp. salt

Directions:

1. Place butter in a microwave-safe bowl then melts the butter.
2. Place chopped mushrooms in a food processor then add eggs, almond flour, and cheddar cheese.
3. Season with salt and pepper then pour melted butter into the food processor. Process until mixed.
4. Transfer to a silicone loaf pan then spread evenly.
5. Preheat an Air Fryer to 375°F (191°C).
6. Place the loaf pan on the Air Fryer's rack then cook for 15 minutes.
7. Once it is done, remove from the Air Fryer then let it cool.
8. Cut the mushroom loaf into slices then serve.
9. Enjoy!

Nutritional Information:

Calories: 365, Fat: 34.6g, Protein: 10.4g, Carbs: 4.4g

Zucchini Parmesan Bites

Servings: 4

Ingredients:

- 4 medium zucchinis
- 1 c. grated coconuts
- 1-tbsp. Italian seasoning
- 2 tbsps. butter
- ½ c. grated Parmesan cheese
- 1 egg

Directions:

1. Allow the butter to melt in a microwave then cool.
2. Peel the zucchinis then cut into halves.
3. Discard the seeds then grate the zucchinis. Place in a bowl.
4. Add grated coconuts, Italian seasoning, melted butter, egg, and Parmesan cheese to the bowl. Mix well.
5. Shape the zucchini mixture into small balls forms then set aside.
6. Preheat an Air Fryer to 400°F (204°C).
7. Place a rack in the Air Fryer then arrange the zucchini balls on it.
8. Cook the zucchini balls for 10 minutes then remove from heat.
9. Serve and enjoy.

Nutritional Information:

Calories: 225, Fat: 17.9g, Protein: 9g, Carbs: 10.6g

Minty Pumpkin Cheese Bombs

Servings: 4

Ingredients:

- ¾ lb. pumpkin
- ¼ c. chopped onion
- ¼ c. chopped parsley
- 2 tsps. chopped mint leaves
- ¼ c. almond flour
- 2 tbsps. butter
- 1 tsp. thyme
- 1½ tbsp. mustard
- ½ tsp. salt
- ½ tsp. pepper
- ¼ lb. mozzarella cheese
- 1 egg
- 1 c. roasted pecans

Directions:

1. Peel the pumpkin then cut into cubes.
2. Place the cubed pumpkin in a food processor then process until smooth.
3. Transfer the smooth pumpkin to a bowl then add chopped onion, parsley, mint leaves, and flour.
4. Pour melted butter into the bowl then season with thyme, mustard, salt, and pepper. Mix until combined.
5. Shape the pumpkin mixture into small balls the fill each ball with Mozzarella cheese.
6. Arrange the pumpkin balls on a tray then refrigerate for 15 minutes.
7. Meanwhile, place the roasted pecans in a food processor then process until smooth and becoming crumbles. Set aside.
8. In a separate bowl, crack the egg then using a fork stir until incorporated.
9. Preheat an Air Fryer to 400°F (204°C).
10. Take the pumpkin bowl out of the refrigerator then dip in the egg.
11. Roll the pumpkin balls in the pecan crumbles then arrange on the Air Fryer's rack.
12. Cook the pumpkin balls for 12 minutes then remove from heat.
13. Serve and enjoy warm.

Nutritional Information:

Calories: 438, Fat: 41.3g, Protein: 12g, Carbs: 9.9g

Avocado Sticks with Garlic Butter

Servings: 6

Ingredients:

- 2 avocados
- 1 c. almond flour
- 2 tsps. black pepper
- 4 egg yolks
- 1½ tbsps. water
- ¼ tsp. salt
- 1 c. butter
- 2 tsps. minced garlic
- ¼ c. chopped parsley
- 1 tbsp. lemon juice

Directions:

1. Place butter in a mixing bowl then adds minced garlic, chopped parsley, and lemon juice to the bowl.
2. Using an electric mixer mix until smooth and fluffy.
3. Transfer the garlic butter to a container with a lid then store in the fridge.
4. Peel the avocados then cut into wedges. Set aside.
5. Put the egg yolks in a mixing bowl then pour water into it.
6. Season with salt and black pepper then stir until incorporated.
7. Take an avocado wedge then roll in the almond flour.
8. Dip in the egg mixture then returns back to the almond flour. Roll until the avocado wedge is completely coated. Repeat with the remaining avocado wedges.
9. Preheat an Air Fryer to 400°F (204°C).
10. Arrange the coated avocado wedges in the Air Fryer basket then cook for 8 minutes or until golden.
11. Remove from the Air Fryer then arrange on a serving dish.
12. Serve with garlic butter then enjoy right away.

Nutritional Information:

Calories: 340, Fat: 33.8g, Protein: 4.5g, Carbs: 8.5g

Cinnamon Chocolate Churros

Servings: 6

Ingredients:

- ¼ c. butter
- ½ c. warm water
- ½ c. almond flour
- 2 eggs
- 2½ tsps. cinnamon
- ¼ c. semi-sweet chocolate chips
- 2 tbsps. almond milk

Directions:

1. Place water and butter in a saucepan then bring to boil.
2. Once it is boiled, add almond flour to the saucepan then stir until becoming a soft dough.
3. Wait until the dough is soft then add eggs to the dough.
4. Using an electric mixer mix until fluffy.
5. Transfer the fluffy dough to a piping bag then set aside.
6. Preheat an Air Fryer to 380°F (193°C).
7. Pipe several pieces of 3-inch-long dough in the Air Fryer then cook for 10 minutes.
8. Remove the churros from the Air Fryer then repeat with the remaining dough.
9. Meanwhile, place semi-sweet chocolate chips in a microwave-safe bowl. Melt the butter in the microwave.
10. Pour almond milk into the melted chocolate then stir until incorporated.
11. Arrange the churros on a serving dish then drizzle melted chocolate over the churros.
12. Sprinkle cinnamon on top then serve.
13. Enjoy.

Nutritional Information:

Calories: 194, Fat: 18.3g, Protein: 4.1g, Carbs: 5g

Almond Coconut Cheesecake

Servings: 8

Ingredients:

- ¾ c. almond flour
- ¾ c. coconut flour
- ½ c. grated coconut
- ¾ c. butter
- 3 c. cream cheese
- 1 c. sour cream
- 5 tbsps. Stevia
- 4 eggs
- 1 tsp. lemon zest

Directions:

1. Prepare a spring-form pan that fits the Air Fryer.
2. Allow butter to melt in the microwave then combine with almond flour, coconut flour, and grated coconut. Mix until becoming dough.
3. Place the dough in the prepared spring-form pan then spread evenly.
4. Press to the bottom of the spring-form pan then store in the fridge.
5. Meanwhile, place cream cheese in a mixing bowl then using an electric mixer beat the cream cheese until soft and fluffy.
6. Add sour cream, stevia, eggs, and lemon zest to the bowl then beat again until incorporated and fluffy.
7. Remove the spring-form pan from the fridge then pour the filling over the base. Spread evenly.
8. Preheat an Air Fryer to 180°F (82°C).
9. Place the spring-form pan in the Air Fryer then cook for 15 minutes.
10. Remove the cheesecake from the Air Fryer then let it cool.
11. Once the cheesecake is cool, store in the fridge for at least 6 hours.
12. Serve and enjoy cold.

Nutritional Information:

Calories: 463, Fat: 46.8g, Protein: 8.3g, Carbs: 4.7g

Conclusion

Let's face it. A good diet enriched with all the proper nutrients is our best shot of achieving an active metabolism and efficient lifestyle. A lot of people think that the Keto diet is simply for people who are interested in losing weight. You will find that it is quite the opposite. This type of diet includes heart-healthy fats like fish, olive oil and nuts while limiting sugars and processed grains to reduce or eliminate your risk of heart diseases. There are intense keto diets where only 5 percent of the diet comes from carbs, 20 percent is from protein, and 75 percent is from fat. But even a modified version of this which involves consciously choosing foods low in carbohydrate and high in healthy fats is good enough.

Thanks for reading this book. I hope it has provided you with enough insight to get you going. Don't put off getting started. The sooner you begin this diet, the sooner you'll start to notice an improvement in your health and well-being.

Furthermore, I hope you get to enjoy all the healthy recipes in this book. Having said that, the next step is to experiment with the different recipes. Enjoy the journey!

Peter Bragg

Made in the USA
Columbia, SC
04 November 2019

82629912R00104